# THE IDEAL BUSINESS FORMULA

# THE IDEAL BUSINESS FORMULA

## How to Build Your IDEAL Business Around Your IDEAL Life.

### By PAT RIGSBY

CelebrityPress®
Winter Park, Florida

# What Others Are Saying About
## *THE IDEAL BUSINESS FORMULA*

*"If you're looking to build a business that is rewarding in every way, Pat is the man that can help you. He'll give you a proven formula for personal and professional success."*

~ Lewis Howes
  New York Times Best-selling Author®

*"Pat Rigsby is the perfect mentor for entrepreneurs. He's not only very successful, but he's achieved that success both the wrong way—suffering from overworking, stress, and burnout— and a more sustainable approach with more balance. The IDEAL Business Formula is a blueprint for a better approach to business—and life."*

- Adam Bornstein
  New York Times Best-selling Author®

*"This book is a MUST for anyone who wants a more fulfilling business. If you want to enjoy your business more and create more IMPACT in the universe, Pat gives you the blueprint with his IDEAL Business Formula book. Definitely a MUST read for any fitness or wellness professional looking for more business development and personal growth."*

~ Todd Durkin
  Author, *The WOW BOOK* & The *IMPACT Body Plan*
  Trainer, NBC STRONG
  Member, Under Armour Performance Training Team

*"After working with Pat Rigsby and many of his successful clients in the health and wellness industry for more than a decade, I convinced Pat that he had to share his simple, practical, yet profound business processes and strategies with the rest of the business world. He finally relented and wrote this book. If you want to make your first 6 figures in business, or want to break through to your next 7 figures, this book is the best place to start."*

~ Nick Nanton
  5-Time Emmy® Award-Winning Director
  Wall Street Journal Best-selling Author® of *StorySelling*

*"Starting a business is challenging. Managing growth of that business is even more challenging. Establishing the lifestyle that you want that actually includes that business is nearly impossible. If there's anyone who can show you how, it's Pat Rigsby—and that's why this book is a must read. As you read it you'll find yourself nodding your head and asking 'Why didn't I think of that?' "*

~ Eric Cressey

*"There are countless generic business resources that may assist you in developing a profitable business. Where Pat differentiates himself from all the others is that not only is he the model guide to profitability (he's done it himself more than once), but he stands alone as the leader in how to build the perfect business for YOU. The IDEAL Business Formula provides the framework for creating a successful business without creating a monster that steals away all of the important things. You'll learn how to keep everything in its place to overcome the obstacles preventing you from creating a unique, high-production business, and how to design, create, and master the process of building your IDEAL life."*

~ Bill Hartman

*"Pat Rigsby has one of the best minds for business, merging the often challenging concepts of business design, effective marketing, and strategic long-term planning. His new book takes that a step further. Many entrepreneurs are stuck in the day to day treading water and hoping for that one magical day where it all pays off. The IDEAL Business Formula helps put you in a position to succeed by assuring you are thinking in both the short and long term. This is something that doesn't come naturally for most people. I am fortunate to have worked with Pat throughout the many stages of my personal online business as well as my brick and mortar gym. His mentorship has helped me build my IDEAL Life and Business."*

~ Mike Reinold

*"Why should you read this book? Because you don't want to just survive in business like most do—existing in the gray twilight of mediocrity. You want to thrive. And Pat Rigsby shows you the exact formula for doing that. In The Art of War, Sun Tzu said, 'Tactics without strategy is the noise before defeat.' Those eight words beautifully summarize exactly why so many business owners are just surviving, stressed out and anxious. Pat knows strategy comes first. And he teaches you the ultimate strategy: how to create your IDEAL Business. A business that serves you, not enslaves you. For over a decade, I've watched Pat intentionally, thoughtfully and strategically grow a dominant, lucrative "Category of One" business. I've seen how he prioritizes family and lifestyle over work—and how that makes him richer, not poorer. How it makes him more focused, present and effective in everything he does. And how that creates for him the freedom so many entrepreneurs pay lip service to, but never really realize. Pat has truly mastered the game of small business. He actually gets to have his cake and eat it too. And when you read this book you'll quickly discover it's not luck, accident or fluke. It's by design—it's formulaic. A formula you can follow to produce the business and life you want most."*

~ Eric Ruth
  founder LocalByReferral.com

*"Pat lays out in detail the essentials of building an IDEAL Business that results in an ideal life. Too often authors bring a half-baked concepts that haven't been proven and tested, Pat is exactly the opposite. Through stories, examples, and proof, he shows you the true requirements of building a life and business you love. A business that serves clients to the best of your ability and results in their growth and your wealth."*

~ Paul Evans
   www.PaulEvans.com

*"Pat Rigsby, in his new book The IDEAL Business Formula, shares his proven model to increase customers and revenue, while also creating systems that help you scale your business and create a personal lifestyle. Pat is the REAL DEAL!"*

~ Kyle Wilson
   Founder Jim Rohn Int., Your Success Store and KyleWilson.com

# ACKNOWLEDGEMENTS

No book becomes a reality through the work of just the author. This is particularly true with the IDEAL Business Formula. I gratefully acknowledge the inspiration and help of the following people; this book would never have been published without you.

Holly—thank you for your support and partnership in business and, more importantly, in life.

Tyler and Alex—thank you for serving as the motivation to make the shift from working to creating the IDEAL Business.

My parents—thank you to my mom, Linda, for being a never ending source of support and to my dad, Ray, for displaying the work ethic that I learned was necessary for business success.

Jeff Ramey—thanks for being both my best friend and my biggest role model.

Many thanks to the people on my team responsible for the "heavy lifting" of getting this from concept into print: Matt, Amy & Denise.

Thank you to all of my coaching clients who have committed to building your own IDEAL Business. It's beyond the scope of this section of the book to thank you each individually, but that doesn't lessen my gratitude for your contribution and commitment.
And thank you to the leaders and friends who have helped me along the way. Professionals like Chris Poirier, Nick Nanton, Jack Dicks, Pat Beith, Eric Cressey, Pete Dupuis, Mike Robertson,

Bill Hartman, Fred Zoller, Mike Reinold, Carrie Wilkerson, Eric Ruth, Luka Hocevar, Kyle Wilson, Scott Rawcliffe, John Berardi, Adam Bornstein, Rick Streb, Justin Yule, Sam Bakhtiar and John Spencer Ellis.

# CONTENTS

# FOREWORD

## BY CARRIE WILKERSON AND
## MIKE ROUSSELL, PhD

*Carrie Wilkerson*

In 1998 my husband and I adopted siblings, a brother and sister, ages two years and eight months respectively. Instantly, we were parents. Instantly, the career I'd worked for (and loved) was less important. Instantly, I wanted to be home, to be a mom, to be the stability that these babies had never had.

I did not have an ounce of business training. I did not have a big world-changing or wealth-building idea. I did not have any capital, product, support or even any spare time. (Instant babies, remember?)

What I did have was a burning desire to create cash using my brain or skills. What I did have was a firm set of core values that I suspected I could keep intact if I created my own business. What I did have was 'more month than money' so I HAD to make it work, no matter what! Oh, how I wish I'd known Pat Rigsby then!

This book didn't exist then, and there were very scarce resources on how to create a business that respected who you were and how you lived. There were plenty of books, infomercials, emails and products about how to create massive income and passive income, how to develop xyz product or pathway, and how to copycat this guru or that...but there was nothing about looking in the mirror, at your calendar, at your family photo, and your priorities and building from what you wanted to reflect.

Fast-forward to now, and you do the math...I've been a business builder a very long time. I've added two more kids, miraculously stayed married (bless his heart), and generated my own income since that first decision. But I've made major mistakes. I checked emails during football games, recitals, and plays, and I wasn't fully present when I could have been. I also flat out did work I resented because I wasn't working wisely or respecting my own 'guardrails.'

Now, I'm smarter. I've taken Pat's workshops, read his materials, and valued our relationship for over ten years. He doesn't just have ideas. He hasn't just 'seen' things work. He lives and breathes what he speaks.

I've been fortunate enough to watch this transition in his life. While I've seen wannabees and could-have-beens come and go, Pat has hung in there, learned and applied, and stood fast for his family and his integrity.

He's come in to teach my clients and I point others in his direction often. Quite simply, I trust him.

His family has been in my home, we've met mid-street at Disney World and we're a testament that not only does the IDEAL Business respect your family and your time, but relationships are important too.

If you believe that profit is king, that prominence is queen and that people are just stepping stones to get where you want to go...this isn't the book for you. However, if you suspect that you can build a meaningful business with radical profitability while keeping your family and building some amazing relationships along the way...then keep reading because Pat is your guy and this is your book.

Get out your highlighter and ink pen. Have your sticky notes ready...your life and business are about to change.

Carrie Wilkerson
Speaker, Author & Consultant
CarrieWilkerson.com

***

*Mike Roussell, PhD*

When I first graduated from Penn State with my PhD in nutrition I had a decision to make. My wife and I had three young children (one only a couple weeks old). What was the next step in my professional life going to be?

Take an academic job researching and teaching at a smaller school with limited budgets and resources?

Find a postdoctoral fellowship and be essentially a glorified graduated student for another two to four years as I built up my resume in order to be a competitive applicant for a tier one research university (nothing about that was attractive to me).

Perhaps I should find a job in the "industry" which paid well... but that healthy compensation came at a price—the "golden handcuffs" that ensured you sang the company's song.

To be honest, none of these sounded appealing to me. It wasn't my passion. I was driven by my love of science but also my love for entrepreneurship. I was closing in on 30 and had been in school my entire life. If I wasn't going to do what I truly wanted to do now, then when? If I wasn't willing to bet on myself then what was the point of all those years of study?

I have always envisioned a different work-life than most PhDs. At Penn State they call my career choice "an alternative option."

19

In this book that you are about to read, Pat calls it the IDEAL Business (but it is really, as he also calls it, the IDEAL Life).

So what did I choose? I chose to bet on myself. I purchased a folding table, put it on four cinderblocks and worked from a standup desk in the spare bedroom in our 1000 square ft. home. When I started out I didn't really know what I was doing, but I knew how to work, network, and build relationships. So that's what I did.

As I read the *The* IDEAL *Business Formula*, I found myself wishing that I had this book when I started out. It is a more concise, more effective, and flat-out better version of the playbook that I developed from years of trial and error. A playbook which took me from a that spare bedroom in central Pennsylvania to building myself into a nationally known nutrition strategist and advisor to Men's Health magazine, numerous professional athletes, celebrities, and high-powered executives...all on my own terms.

My approach was fueled by hustle and caffeine. Fortunately, Pat outlines for you a slightly more elegant approach. An approach that still requires hustle (and probably caffeine), but one that understands you don't need to be everything to everyone while also being a regular on the *Today* Show to live your IDEAL Life.

In fact, it is a lot simpler than you think.

Pat's approach will show you step by step how to map out, work towards, and live your IDEAL Business—whatever it may be. Creating and running your IDEAL Business isn't about drinking margaritas on a hammock in the Caribbean (it can be if you want that), but instead it is about being very clear about what you want (and don't want) in your life, what it takes to get it, and then relentlessly executing to achieve it. *The* IDEAL *Business Formula* isn't your guide to the easy life, but instead the good life. Whether you enjoy lounging at Disney World so much that the cast members know you by name and how you like your coffee (like Pat), or you like spending the summer months split between cabins in the woods of the northeast and cottages on the beaches of Maine (like me), *The* IDEAL *Business Formula* will be your trusted blueprint for making it happen.

This book is not full of quick fixes and lists of the top ways to growth hack your way to stardom. Instead, Pat shares how he has used tried and true marketing and relationship-sustaining tactics and adopted them for solo or small business entrepreneurs that want to live life on their own terms.

Autonomy is the greatest asset you have. This book will show you how to achieve it—if you are willing to be a producer and put in the work.

Mike Roussell, PhD

# PREFACE

Imagine if you had spent the last 15 years speaking with thousands of fitness and wellness entrepreneurs. In the process, you realize you've probably logged more time in conversations with these business owners than anyone else in the world. You'd hear stories of brave fit pros putting everything on the line for their dreams...only to struggle for years on end. Then, in piecing all these stories together, you'd notice some 'big data' patterns emerging most others miss.

You'd discover a universal type of language:

*"I need to earn more personal income for the time and effort I'm putting into my business."*

*"I don't have enough time for myself or my family."*

*"I feel like my business 'owns' me."*

*"I'm burned out."*

*"I don't enjoy owning my business anymore."*

Can you relate? I certainly can.

In fact, you should know I've experienced every one of those negative emotions at one time or another. You see, I've built over 25 different businesses ranging from award-winning franchises with hundreds of locations to small online businesses. And along the way, I've felt like there were never enough hours in the day.

I know the personal pain of feeling like my efforts were going unrewarded. I know the seductive feeling of success is just one more business, one more promotion, or one more employee away. But through all the madness, I discovered a vital truth.

The passion in which I was pursuing success—the adrenalin addiction I was operating under—was all wrong.

I was in constant pursuit and hunger for 'more'...more revenue, more clients, more franchisees...more, more, more. No matter how much success I achieved, I always felt the target could be a little bigger...pushed out a bit further...and just out of reach so that I would be forced to chase it.

Then one day, when the pressure cooker of life wouldn't let my health take it anymore, I asked myself a question. And that question led me down a completely different path—a path that ultimately inspired this book:

"What is business success for me?"

Not success according to some arbitrary gross revenue target. Not based on being recognized in the Entrepreneur Franchise 500, or in the Inc. 5000. Not based on how many franchisees I added or products I sold.

No. No. No...success, for me, couldn't be any of that.

Instead, I had to find out...

"What changes must take place for me to have the professional impact I want...while enjoying a personal lifestyle I crave?"

My answer evolved into what I've coined The IDEAL Business. And that's what I've built.

Today, my work schedule could not be any more different. I have the flexibility to coach my son's baseball team. I can disconnect from work most evenings and weekends. And I take more time off annually than I could in the entire decade leading up to this shift.

Yet my impact has never been more significant, and my income is 3X more than it was when I was running two franchises and a host of other businesses. And I love my work pretty much every day. Sure, there are challenging moments. Like you, I tolerate quarterly taxes and all the rest of the stuff we have to navigate as business owners. But instead of enjoying 20% of my time at work, now I enjoy more than 90%. So—yes—I've built my IDEAL Business...

But this book isn't about MY business. This book is about what it takes to build YOUR IDEAL Business.

It's time someone showed you, step-by-step, how to build the business you want to own. This book is vastly different from any other business book you've read. That's because this book is not a blueprint for building a clone of someone else's business. Nor is this book designed to address a single component of business success. It's not about any of that kind of stuff.

Instead, this book is about you—100% you and your IDEAL Business—and what you want out of it.

Now, before you dive in, I will tell you up front there is no magic bullet or secret formula for building your IDEAL Business. Forget all of those over-the-top claims that have distorted people's expectations of what business success should look like or how it's attained. What I will tell you, however, is that creating your IDEAL Business (or re-engineering your current business so that it becomes IDEAL), is not complicated. In many ways, this approach will take you back to the basics and ask you to use time-tested concepts and principles that will yield sustainable success. In fact, I'm going to ask you to rethink how you go about achieving success and consider adopting what I suspect will be a simpler path to achieving your goals. And I fully expect that creating and operating your IDEAL Business will likely feel less like 'hard work' than what you've been experiencing until now.

Now this may sound intangible at the moment, but don't worry, things will become clearer before you know it. I've gone to great lengths to simplify the formula you are about to read. That's because building your IDEAL Business provides you an operating system for achieving personal and professional success. The success that has not only worked for me, but for hundreds of my clients in building the business that they want.

Here's the bottom line: You can have the business that you want. The plan that will help you go from where you are today to having your IDEAL Business is spelled out for you on the following pages. Now it's up to you.

While you can't sleepwalk your way through the creation of your IDEAL Business...if you're willing to make some small changes in the way you think, and the actions you take, I promise you can change your life. It's that simple. You'll begin by eliminating the parts of your business you're eager to escape. And you'll work your way through the process until you arrive at a place that looks remarkably like your IDEAL Business—a business you may have thought wasn't possible.

To make the process of building your IDEAL Business easy as possible, I've included a variety of resources at TheIDEALBusinessBook.com. Please, use them! They are for your own good.

This book (and the tools I've provided to support you), can be life changing if put into action. I know they have been for me and I am confident that creating your IDEAL Business can have just as much impact for you.

Let's get you started!

INTRODUCTION

# THE HOLIDAY THAT WASN'T

What better way to spend a family Thanksgiving than with Mickey Mouse? Disney World may or may not be your ideal vacation, but my wife and I love the "most magical place on earth;" which is why we spend the holiday weekend at Disney World every year. Our boys love the giant theme park and all the good times it offers, and we love to treat them to those experiences. To tell the truth, it's fun for us grown-ups as well.

However in 2013, Thanksgiving was different. I woke up early, before my wife and boys, because I had to participate in something that was very far from my idea of a good time. On any other day, I wouldn't have had a problem with it, but not this day. Not when I was supposed to be relaxing with my family on a holiday vacation.

Instead, I had to go down to the hotel lobby with my laptop and jump on a call that my business partner had scheduled for us and other members of our leadership team—yes, on Thanksgiving morning. I had to refocus on the business matters that I had come to Disney World to forget about for a few days. That meeting (and the way I felt about it) was the first real indicator that my life was becoming something I didn't want it to be.

For the past decade, I had been working 24/7 to build a successful career as an entrepreneur in the fitness industry. That meant I had been in constant hustle mode for ten years—beginning with my personal training business and constantly growing from there. At first, I was in the gym every morning, noon, night, and weekends. If you name it, I was probably at the gym. Along the way, I managed to squeeze in some time for my wedding, but because I had married somebody who was in the same business, the number of work hours didn't really drop. Instead, both of us spent *all* our time at the gym!

Her four-year-old son, now my stepson, got swept up in our professional pursuits as well. His preschool bus would pick him up *at the gym* in the morning and bring him back afterward. We had a little area set up in the back for him where he could watch movies and play so he could have his own "chill" time until we headed home for his bedtime. About all we did at home was sleep.

Why was I so consumed with work? Well, I really didn't get started as an entrepreneur until I was thirty-two. Before that, I had been a baseball coach at a state university. My initial career choice didn't leave me swimming in money, so at thirty-two I set out to make up for lost time. I wanted to take care of my new family and wanted to make sure we had a comfortable future ahead of us.

Fortunately for our son, my wife and I were able to shift much of her business to an online model about three years into our marriage, which left me as the only "gym rat" in the family. Only now, because my whole ambition was to earn as much income as possible, I had expanded my operation to two gyms and was spending a lot of time on the road. The facilities were about two hours apart. Between my working hours and driving hours, life was really getting insane.

Something had to give.

As I still hadn't achieved most of my entrepreneurial goals, I made a conscious decision to move in the direction my wife was going with her business. If I could sell informational products, deliver coaching to other small business owners, and get into licensing and franchising, I could grow my business and our income without having to be physically present everywhere I was planting seeds.

That seemed to be working out until my wife and I had a child. By this time I was around forty and had successfully refocused my businesses so that I didn't have to always be traveling. I could supervise most of my "mini-empire" virtually, which meant I could be more involved in raising our kids. I felt I had put enough "sweat equity" into my business to have earned the right to experience a little bit of the work-family balance I craved so much.

But, once again, I was a victim of my own success.

My ability to control my time faded quickly. As my businesses grew, my responsibilities kept snowballing. I was suddenly doing a lot of stuff I wasn't all that excited about. I was looking after almost forty employees, I had a couple hundred franchisees with their own individual needs, and suddenly I was in charge of a huge operation that didn't leave much room for the most important people in my life: my wife and our boys. I was spending so much time trying to sync up with other people's schedules that my own personal schedule went up in flames. There were constant conflicts between what I wanted to do and what I actually *had* to do to keep things running smoothly.

Now, I'm as far from an egomaniac as you might imagine, but I kept thinking to myself, *I started all these businesses to achieve MY goals, not everyone else's*. I didn't want to say my life and work was all about me—but *some* of it should be, right? I mean life's too short. Why would I sacrifice what was most important in my life just to become a hamster that keeps running so that its wheel never stops?

Yet, at the same time, I still felt the drive to achieve. I wanted to see my name on the Entrepreneur Franchise 500 list. I wanted to be recognized in the business community as a leader. And, of course, I wanted to create sustainable success for my family and myself.

I also wanted to be a good dad and husband, as well as serve as an excellent example to my kids. If my kids grew up only caring about their careers because of what they watched me do with my life, I certainly wouldn't be happy about that. And ultimately neither would they.

Eventually, I did begin to win awards and have my name mentioned in magazines. I found less and less fulfillment in those recognitions. Instead, I felt more and more conflicted about the path I was on. Did I want to feel guilty when I was out in the yard playing catch with my son? No, but I did. A lot of other people's livelihoods were tied up in my operation, and I felt that responsibility keenly. I constantly felt that tension. When my son and I were playing catch, there was always the thought in the back of my mind that I could have been doing something productive to help my businesses keep thriving. That thought made just being a dad who was playing with his kids seem… frivolous.

Then that Thanksgiving morning happened. Why did I need to be on a business call on a morning when millions of other Americans were enjoying some well-deserved time off with their families? I didn't. That realization was a tipping point for me.

I made a vow that I was going to start a brand-new business created with a set of "guardrails" firmly in place so that I wouldn't have to constantly battle for a spare minute to be with my wife and kids. (I'll be talking about how to apply your own guardrails later in this book.) Over the next year, I started to research how other successful people who had achieved more balance in their lives approached business differently—how they navigated their role as a leader without doing so at the expense of their family life or whatever other personal interests they might have.

Result? Today I'm happier, I earn more money, and I work far less than at any other time in my professional life. In every category I've just mentioned, that increase has been by at least a multiple of two.

Now I can look back and see I spent far too much time playing by other people's rules of what success should be. For me to really win, I had to let go of those preconceived ideas and play by my own rules—what I call "The IDEAL Business Rules" in this book. When I saw I could create a business based on *my* life goals, built with firm boundaries in place, that's when I really transformed my life into something that was ideal for me and my family.

I want to help you do the same. I want you to achieve your IDEAL Life, combining professional success with personal satisfaction in a way that most people think is impossible. The reality is, it's easier that you think. I discovered that when you allow yourself the freedom to create the future you want, you suddenly unlock possibilities you never would have seen otherwise.

This book is designed to help any entrepreneur or professional find those possibilities and transform them into reality. I'll be sharing the hard-earned experience and knowledge that I've gained through my own process of discovering my IDEAL Business Rules. These are proven practices that have worked for me, and I think they'll work for you. At the very least, maybe they'll inspire you to come up with a few rules of your own to help you get where you want to go.

But this book isn't only about possibilities. It's also about dealing with cold, hard realities that every business must face on a day-to-day basis. That's why I'm also going to share a lot of commonsense advice, tailored specifically to the entrepreneurial mind-set. All of the advice I've included is practical, and it is informed by my viewpoint that doing business doesn't have to be an endless grind that leads nowhere. Hard work can take you to the next level if you allow yourself to dream and direct your energy toward the right targets.

Ready to take the first step toward your IDEAL Life? Then turn the page (or swipe to it, if you're checking out the e-version) and start reading...

# CHAPTER 1

# THE IDEAL LIFE

Americans work hard, harder than almost anyone else in the world. According to the International Labour Organization, we work 137 more hours per year than people in Japan, 260 more hours per year than those in Britain, and 499 more hours per year than those in France. Furthermore, overwork is an equal opportunity offender: A majority of both male and female workers are on the job for more than forty hours per week. I'd be willing to bet the hours for entrepreneurs and anyone who owns their own business are a lot more than that.

Of course, all this hard work does pay off. The United States ranks at the top in terms of prosperity with the highest gross domestic product per capita. You know what we're not number one in, however? Being happy.

Among the countries in the world, we're only number sixteen in terms of overall well-being and all the way down at the twenty-sixth slot for life enjoyment, according to a Gallup World poll. Shouldn't we be reaping more personal rewards for working so hard?

Now, don't get me wrong; I have nothing against hard work. As a matter of fact, hard work and I have been companions throughout my entire adult life. I've started more than twenty-five businesses and have been fortunate enough to have seven of them generate more than a million dollars in revenue. That didn't happen all by itself, but it did require working countless early mornings and late nights, not to mention weekends and holidays.

That's life for most entrepreneurs, and it often leads to a chronic condition that is of our own making called *anhedonia*. I didn't make up that word. It's for real. The dictionary definition is "the inability to experience pleasure from activities usually found enjoyable, e.g., exercise, hobbies, music, or social interactions."

I would only modify that meaning for our purposes to point out that it's not that we *can't* enjoy these activities; it's that we never allow ourselves the time to participate in them. That's because of a side effect our anhedonia causes: a severe case of tunnel vision. We get to a point where we see nothing but our businesses and all the things we must do to keep them growing and thriving.

For entrepreneurs, anhedonia usually worsens over the years because we're afraid to seek a cure. We're frightened that the minute we attempt to mix in personal pleasure with our professional demands we'll lose our focus, our companies will crash, and our employees will end up out on the street. And so might we, for that matter.

It's a normal reaction. After all, the entrepreneur's biggest fear in life is failure. We don't work for others, so we can't rely on anyone else to keep us afloat. We must depend on ourselves. Honestly, we like that state of affairs. In fact, most of us became entrepreneurs so we wouldn't have to answer to anyone else.

However, independence comes at a cost, and that cost is often not enjoying our lives to the extent that we should—or sometimes not enjoying our lives at all. We get addicted to work and avoid giving ourselves permission for any kind of ongoing enjoyment— except, perhaps, for the excitement we feel when our businesses reach new levels of success. We neglect families. We let go of personal passions and pursuits. We draw a great big box around our daily existence, and inside that box is only work, work, and more work.

That brings me to the first of my IDEAL Business Rules:

## IDEAL BUSINESS RULE #1: DON'T WORK HARD JUST SO YOU CAN END UP WORKING HARDER.

Frankly, we can lose who we are if work consumes our entire existence. Here are a few danger signs that your business has taken away too much of your life:

- You try to go to the movies, but end up out in the lobby the whole time just checking your email and returning phone calls.
- You have your assistant schedule a call/time to catch up with your mom.
- After you finish dinner, you have no idea what you ate because you were completely focused on how to implement your next marketing campaign.
- You cancel your climb to the peak of Mt. Everest because you find out there's no internet up there.

Okay, that last one might be a bit of an exaggeration, but not by much. I know because I used to have my own severe case of constant overwork.

There was a time when I thought it was unthinkable to put my personal life on equal footing with my professional life. When you're running the show, when everything is on your shoulders, you're afraid to shift priorities even for a second. The thing is, your personal happiness shares a common truth with your professional success: If you don't protect it and nurture it, nobody is going to do it for you.

As entrepreneurs, we can achieve a life-work balance that works. After all, we tend to be goal-oriented people with plenty of drive, so why wouldn't we want to put those qualities to work for ourselves as well as for our businesses? It's simply a matter of creating realistic targets for ourselves on both sides, personal and professional, and uncovering ways to achieve those targets.

Sure, it's a little too simplistic to just holler, "You can have it all!" Life's a little too messy for that kind of broad generalization. But, I have discovered for myself that entrepreneurial success and personal happiness aren't mutually exclusive. As a matter of fact, they can get along quite nicely.

The late Senator Paul Tsongas once made the memorable remark, "Nobody on his deathbed ever said, 'I wish I had spent more time at the office.'" Think about that. Then think about your own life in ten or twenty years—or even thirty or forty years. Think about what you'll have to look back on as well as look forward to. Do you want it all to be about work?

If you don't take the time to build a life along with your business, regret could easily be your legacy. Sure, you might end up with all the money you desire...but what good is a full bank account if your life is empty?

*"Be careful what you wish for."* That's another quote I love to hang on to. It came from the direct marketing legend, Dan Kennedy, when he was warning people about creating a success for yourself that you grow to hate. That's exactly what I did before I realized I could re-engineer that success, and my business, to make it what I wanted it to be: a business that allows me to reach my professional goals and fulfills me personally.

You can make that happen for yourself too. I know you can, because I've done it. Let's talk about how to you can create the kind of life balance that so few entrepreneurs get to experience.

### Knowing Where You're Going

Your first step in this process is to shift your mind-set and set a new direction.

The late Stephen Covey, in his critically acclaimed, best-selling book, *The Seven Habits of Highly Effective People* (a favorite of entrepreneurs, by the way), cited the very first habit of the seven as "Begin with the end in mind."

I'm certainly not going to quibble with that because it makes a whole lot of sense, especially when it comes to the subject of this book. Planning your IDEAL Life, a life that combines personal satisfaction and professional success, must be a very strategic pursuit. It begins with knowing exactly what you're trying to accomplish on a business level.

## IDEAL BUSINESS RULE #2:
## IF YOU DON'T KNOW WHERE YOU'RE GOING, YOU'RE NEVER GOING TO GET THERE.

When you don't have your ultimate goals in mind at the get-go, you make the mistakes I did:

- You build businesses randomly and continuously with a scattershot approach that's more accidental than purposeful.
- You end up hustling constantly trying to keep up with it all, which just transforms your life into a nonstop marathon.
- You never see the finish line, because there is no finish line in your head.

Now, there's no question when you're starting out in your entrepreneurial career that you're going to have to live your life at a very hectic pace. There's a lot to do and a lot to learn because, for the most part, you're going to be doing everything yourself. There's nothing wrong with that, it's the normal course of things. What you can do to make your life easier though is having your goals in mind before you even begin to put the pieces of your business together. I would suggest writing them down so you can refer to them as your business grows.

Think about this. When you get into your car, truck or private jet (there's got to be somebody reading this who has one!), you almost always have a destination in mind. Otherwise, you'll end up traveling in circles and arriving nowhere. Well, it's the same with your professional pursuits. When you don't know where you want to go, you're going to need a lot of luck to end up at a place that makes you happy.

However, when you have an end game in your head from day one, that goal will inform all your decisions. You will shape your own destiny instead of putting yourself at the mercy of fate. Things won't always go in the direction you want, but when the opportunity comes to shift toward the direction you want to go, you'll leap at it.

All because you know what you want.

It's crucial to give your professional goals some real thought from day one. After all, when you craft the IDEAL Business, you've created the conditions to build your IDEAL Life.

Now, let's talk about what an ideal business is all about. Or, as I frame it, an IDEAL Business.

## The Components of the IDEAL Business

What should you have in the mix when it comes to the attributes of your perfect business? Where should your focus be?

When I regrouped and retooled my entrepreneurial goals after my unwelcome Thanksgiving morning wake-up call, I gave those attributes some serious thought. I finally came up with **five distinct qualities** that had to be a part of any business with which I was involved in the future. I'm sure you can come up with others that are particularly important to you, but these five pretty much cover the bases—not only for me, but almost every entrepreneur I know who wants to experience the IDEAL Life.

That IDEAL Life requires the IDEAL Business.

Which brings me to the reason IDEAL is capitalized when I talk about business. IDEAL is an acronym with each letter representing one of those five distinct qualities. When all five are firmly in place, your business goes beyond endless drudgery and ongoing obligations to an exciting endeavor that makes you feel pumped up about what you're doing each and every day. It will take time to make sure all five elements are in play, but once you swing it, you're going to be very glad you put in the effort to make them an integral part of your entrepreneurial life.

Let's go through them, one at a time:

## I = Independence

When you read a list of what character traits most entrepreneurs have in common, "independence" usually tops the list. There's a reason we go into business for ourselves: We don't want to answer to anyone else. Before I became an entrepreneur, I worked for a state university. So much of my job entailed dealing with government bureaucracy, red tape, and budgets. That lack of control continually frustrated me, especially when I could see so many ways to do things better and faster. It would have been easier to try and push a skyscraper over on its side than to actually change over-complicated systems that had grown more and more unwieldy through the years.

That experience made me want to take control of my professional life and become an entrepreneur. Sure, I still have conflicts and obstacles, but I have the ability to choose my own solutions to problems without anyone else telling me it's not "procedure" or how things are supposed to be done. Instead, I get to decide how to tackle challenges. Luckily, I've been pretty successful with those decisions, so I never had any cause to regret going out on my own.

Yet sometimes entrepreneurs still end up fighting for control. For example, Steve Jobs and Bill Gates, the two great technology giants of the modern era, both ended up buying out the partners with whom they started their businesses because they wanted to be completely in charge. Not to compare myself to those two legends, but I, too, had a business partner with whom I ended up parting ways. It happened simply because we had different visions for where we wanted our company to go. Sometimes partnerships work, sometimes they don't—and it's up to you to decide if you're comfortable sharing command. Of course, much of that decision comes down to who the other person is and what they're all about.

Then there are franchise opportunities, a common pursuit for an entrepreneur. The problem there can be that it's hard to put yourself in somebody else's box and play by their rules when you have your own personal goals and your own professional objectives. I've been a franchisee (as well as a franchisor with more than 250 locations), and in this case the franchisors offered a lot of freedom and flexibility in how I could run my franchise. Nonetheless, the basic set-up can feel limiting because you're still implementing someone else's business model, not your own. (Still, you might have to experience the franchise option before you can determine whether it's right for you.)It's all a matter of how much independence you ultimately want. For me, it became an absolute necessity to gain total control of my business dealings. That may be the way you feel as well.

Whichever way you choose to go—solopreneur, partnership, franchisee/franchisor, etc.—having a significant measure of independence is the critical element to your ultimate happiness. How else can you have enough of the control you need to build the life you want?

## D = Distinctive

*A successful business stands out from the pack.*

Think about the reasons you choose a restaurant for dinner.

Maybe you like the atmosphere or the service. Maybe the location or the pricing appeal to you. Or maybe your kids love the puzzles they put on the children's menu. It could be anything. The point is, the eatery *gives you a reason* to want to go there instead of some other place.

If you had not noticed, I didn't even give "the food" as one of those reasons. That's because what makes *your* business special is frequently not about what product or service it provides— rather, *how* it provides it.

Every great business finds a way to be *distinctive*, to offer a unique and attractive quality that creates a positive point of difference from its competition. McDonalds, for example, started out as just another hamburger joint, but its ability to differentiate through speed and consistency helped it take off in a huge way. Successful entrepreneurs always look for a way to make their businesses distinctive and to communicate that distinctiveness in a memorable and impactful way to their potential customers, clients, or patients.

Think about these examples of distinctive businesses:

- A dentist who turns their office into a relaxing spa experience
- An attorney who offers free educational videos and books to educate the local community about the law
- A niche food market that offers the best organic produce in town

Those are the kinds of qualities that raise businesses above the everyday and bring in a regular stream of folks who are ready to pay for the pleasure of patronizing them. People get excited about these special "extras" and will, at the drop of a hat, dump bland, one-size-fits-all companies that don't provide that special "wow" factor one way or the other.

For example, if you're into fitness, you don't want to hear people saying, "Oh, she's just another personal trainer." You want to hear them say something like, "She's the woman who can help you lose weight in no time flat." If you run a restaurant, you don't want people saying, "Oh, it's just another barbecue joint." You want them saying things like, "These guys make the best barbecue tacos you've ever had in your life!" Whatever you want to specialize in, you want to be known for that and capitalize on it.

In short, you want to be a "Category of One." You want to be unique. If possible, you want to be extraordinary. Being distinctive gives your business a purpose as well as a magnetic attraction that will bring in paying customers or patients for years to come.

## E = Enjoyable

As you might have noticed by now, much of this book is dedicated to the concept of enjoying your life. Now, if you can't enjoy your work—the thing that occupies most of your waking hours—your life is going to suffer enormously. That's why the IDEAL Business always has a big enjoyable component.

Let's face it, far more people wake up with the dread of having to go to work rather than being excited that they get to go to work. They tolerate that miserable mind-set because they see their careers as a means to an end (money and security) rather than an exciting, ongoing opportunity to achieve and grow.

When I decided to establish the rules for my own IDEAL Business, I determined that I would be intentional about making sure my professional life always included enjoyment. Sure, I've had ups and downs professionally, but the downs have never been all that low. I've found that what I think of as my *worst* job is often a lot better than many people's *best* jobs!

Enjoyment is a result of how I approach work, in that I have always pursued or created opportunities that tapped into my *passions*. I was always interested in sports and fitness, so it was fun tackling businesses in those arenas. Likewise, entrepreneurship fascinates me, so it's a treat to figure out how to leverage my businesses and make them successful.

It's true that many people take the entrepreneurial route because they want their work life to be enjoyable and *not* tied to a nine-to-five job for someone else. But then they create their own career hell, getting themselves tied down doing a whole bunch of stuff that they don't want to do rather than things they really care about.

I know so many entrepreneurs and business owners who wake up and their first thought is, "I don't want to work today." When *that's* your first thought, you've become a slave to your own business. Yes, work is work, but it doesn't have to be just a job. It can actually be fun if you make enjoyment a priority.

Also, you must *keep* making enjoyment a priority. It's so common for people to love their businesses when they start them; but then, as that business grows, so do their responsibilities. Suddenly they find they're spending all their time administering and supervising; they're spending no time doing the things they love—the things that drove them to start the business in the first place! It's like a chef who opens his own restaurant and discovers, to his horror, that all the headaches of running the place have sucked the joy out of preparing meals.

You don't want to end up tolerating your business, let alone hating it. Instead, your goal should be to feel excited about the challenges your work brings you, even if that means completely changing things up. I had to reboot my businesses to keep the enjoyment factor high, and I'm here to tell you, it *is* possible to sustain an entrepreneurial life that you love.

One final note: Making sure your work is enjoyable isn't about being self-indulgent, self-centered, or elitist. Enjoying what you do helps you achieve more. If something is enjoyable, you're willing to go the extra mile to take it to a higher level. You're more likely to educate yourself on how to become the best in your field and to serve your clients, customers or patients at the highest level.

Loving your work creates an ongoing motivation that doesn't require you read inspirational posters on the wall or pump yourself up with affirmations. It's another critical component of an IDEAL Business.

## A = Authentic

Tom Cruise and Sylvester Stallone have built up some incredible expectations for themselves. On the big screen, they've been regularly portrayed as unstoppable physical specimens that no one dares challenge. When the biggest, scariest dudes you ever saw in your life finally take on these on-screen heroes, they end up getting their butts kicked to the extreme.

Should you be lucky enough to encounter Tom or Sly in person, however, you will most likely have one immediate thought: *Wow. This guy's really... short.*

Of course, movie actors can never live up to their silver screen images. Hollywood knows how to make its stars so much bigger than life that, in person, they're bound to be, well, *smaller.* As an entrepreneur, it's important to avoid that kind of in-person disappointment. You want to be the person your customer base thinks you are.

Imagine if Kentucky Fried Chicken Founder, Colonel Sanders, had been exposed as a vegetarian. Or if you discovered that Warren Buffet was secretly broke. Those kinds of disclosures would surely ruin their images for all time—because they directly clash with their public images.

When you brand your business, you're making certain implicit promises to the public. And it's *you* who is making those promises. You're not a movie actor playing a part; those guys get some leeway. Nobody expects Daniel Craig to really bring down international conspiracies like James Bond does. No, you're a real, live human being, and customers and patients will desert you if you prove to be someone different than the image you project.

That's why, from the start, you need to be authentic. Let's say you start a chain of martial arts studios and present yourself as a black belt master to attract customers to your classes. Let's say the reality is that you couldn't kick through a wall of Jell-O. If those studios take off, are you going to spend the next ten, twenty, or even thirty years trying to keep up this pretense?

Maybe the more important question is, are you going to be *able* to keep up that pretense?

People are quick to see through a phony, so you need to be very, very real. I always have strived for this. When I began doing webinars and speaking engagements, I had to think for a few moments about what I should wear. Should I invest in a bunch of expensive suits and designer ties? Dazzle them with my fashion sense?

For me, deciding what to wear was a reality check. My idea of being formal is wearing a polo shirt; I wouldn't look or act comfortable in those fancier outfits. A suit and tie to me is about as appealing as taking a nap on a bed of nails. So I stayed true to who I was and continue to do so to this day. You may see me in a suit or tux every year or two at a wedding or party…and that might even be a stretch.

Because I've put myself front and center with my information products and daily email newsletter, it's important to me that when people meet me in person, their image of me and the real me match up precisely. I want to be the same guy of whom they're already (hopefully) a fan. Otherwise, I lose at least a little bit of their respect, and over time, that catches up with you.

The good part about authenticity is that if you're already putting into place the first three attributes of IDEAL (Independent, Distinctive, Enjoyable), it's going to be extremely difficult *not* to add "Authentic" to the mix. As a matter of fact, I'd say it's darn near impossible because the business is reflective of your goals, values, and objectives.

**You're always better off being the person you are instead of pretending to be someone else.** Sure, you may study someone you want to emulate, but you must put your own spin on the ball. Even if you love the message of this book, you don't want to *be* me; you need to be you! (Besides, the world doesn't need any more Pat Rigsbys, believe me. One is more than enough for all of us.) The world is always looking for something new, not a pale copy of what's already around and available. Put *your* particular expertise, talents, and personality to work for you. The world will thank you for it.

### L = Lucrative

There's a bottom line to the IDEAL Business: It must be lucrative. Your company must be able to compensate you fairly and provide you with the financial security and the lifestyle you want to enjoy. Otherwise, what's the point?

By lucrative I don't mean that you have a plan to make money— *eventually.* Maybe a year or two? Okay. But you don't want to shortchange your life today. Time is not a renewable resource. You want to be able to enjoy yourself and do the things that make you happy *now*—not just when you retire. That means if you want to take a vacation, you should be able to afford it. To experience an IDEAL Life, you need to be able to pursue your interests and hobbies, whether that means traveling, spending time with your family, or taking a day off to play golf. One of the primary goals of an IDEAL Business is that it affords you the kind of personal, financial, and time freedom and flexibility you desire.

As an entrepreneur, you take more risks than the average person. If you risk more, then the rewards should be bigger. The IDEAL attributes—independent, distinctive, enjoyable, authentic, and lucrative—all go a long way toward feeding into your ultimate success. Later in this book we're going to get more specific about how to upsize your business income and make it as consistent and healthy as possible.

You might not hit all five of the IDEAL qualities right away. There may be times when you put yourself in a position in which somebody else is calling the shots for a while, where you can't fulfill the unique position you staked out, where you are definitely *not* having a good time trying to move the needle, or even when you have to play a little game of pretend to pull something off. It happens, and if it's only for the short term, you may have to grit your teeth and get through it. Even when it comes to making money, it's a truism that all entrepreneurs have ups and downs. The idea of being lucrative may seem like a far-flung fantasy when the money spigot sputters for a few weeks or even a few months. That's life.

Nevertheless, when one or two of them are missing long term, you will feel the void they create. I always knew when one or more of them was missing. That was why I began to apply a litmus test to my life when I was a baseball coach. I understood there were days that were going to be rough, days when I didn't want to go to work. I understood there might be a week or so when I would be discouraged or down about what I had to do for a living. However, if I went through two months of constantly feeling that way...well, then, something had to change. As I've progressed to other businesses, I found myself going back to that litmus test time and time again. If negative feelings were overpowering me for too long, then it was time to take some action and turn things around.

Your window of tolerance might be shorter—or longer. Depends on how much patience you've got and how much light is at the end of that particular tunnel. But if you're experiencing two months of consecutive pain, you've definitely got a flaw in your business approach that you need to correct. Most likely it has a lot to do with at least one of the five IDEAL attributes we've discussed in this chapter.

Even if you don't have all five IDEAL attributes in place right now, you can still focus on making that an ongoing goal. Because when all five *are* in place, they allow you to fully engage with your entrepreneurial efforts in a positive and fulfilling way.

Recently, basketball legend Tim Duncan retired. This five-time NBA champion and two-time league MVP retired after nineteen seasons with one team, the San Antonio Spurs. Not only was he considered to be one of the best power forwards ever to play the game, but he was also giving up a $20 million contract for one more year of play.

Why would you walk away from something at which you're so good? Something that paid you that kind of money? Duncan had a very short answer to that question:

"It wasn't fun anymore."

That sums up this chapter as well as my philosophy behind the IDEAL Business. If it's not fun, you've got to fix it. Life's too short, and there are plenty of other options to pursue. As an entrepreneur, you're fortunate enough to have given yourself the freedom and the ability to pursue them.

# CHAPTER 2

# **THE IDEAL MIND-SET**

A while back, a software start-up entrepreneur hired me as a consultant for the company he founded. He had done a lot of hustling to get it off the ground. It was doing well, but to maintain momentum and keep growing, he had to keep up the frantic pace. We've all been there.

The problem was, this guy had three kids who were growing almost as quickly as his business. He constantly talked about how much he loved them and how important they were, but he never spent much time with them or his wife. As a result, the family seemed to be fraying at the edges. As a consultant who could look at the big picture of his life, the disconnect and tension in his priorities really bothered me.

"You've got to go spend some time with your family," I told him one day. "I don't want to be a part of a business that gets you divorced, even if it ends up selling for eight figures."

He didn't change anything. He was out of town for one daughter's birthday, then out of town for another daughter's birthday. That doubleheader made him realize he had a problem, so he tried to make it up. He took the family somewhere for the weekend. He tried to be there more nights. He told me he thought things were better.

"Well," I replied, "that depends. Here's the real test. Are you present when you're around them, or are you constantly checking your phone for messages and emails? Are you focused on them, or are you still focusing on work?"

He looked at me sheepishly. "Yeah, I sneak away and I do stuff on my phone."

"Well, that's almost as bad as not being there at all," I said.

A lot of entrepreneurs try to justify this kind of behavior by saying things like, "But I'm doing all this for my family!" or, "Yeah, I'm sacrificing some family stuff now, but it's only so we have a great future together."

My response to this kind of rationalization is that your family wants your time now more than they want your money later. Which brings me to my next rule...

## IDEAL BUSINESS RULE #3: YOUR WORK SHOULD ENRICH YOUR LIFE, NOT BE YOUR LIFE.

Your life should be more than work. All work, all the time leads to burn out and exhaustion. That's why it's important to take on what I call "the IDEAL mind-set."

What do I mean by an IDEAL mind-set?

Well, as I hope I made clear in Chapter 1, creating the IDEAL Business requires a purposeful mental shift away from doing "business as usual." An IDEAL mind-set represents the result of that shift and embraces out-of-the-box thinking that will deliver what we desire out of life.

As entrepreneurs, we're all sometimes guilty of having more energy than sense. Whenever we see any kind of opportunity to grow our businesses, we jump at it. Sometimes that short-term action sabotages our long-term aspirations, especially when we don't stop to think through our decisions and actions. That's why I say the most powerful word when it comes to business success is this familiar one:

"No."

So many entrepreneurs are afraid to say that magic two-letter word. It's normal, especially in the early stages when we're young. We're starting out, and frankly, we aren't worried about our future as much as our present. It can be hard enough to pay the bills and make a go of whatever our enterprise happens to be without worrying about whether what we're doing really squares up with our life plan. We just figure if we work hard enough, that alone will solve all our problems. But when we constantly chase after the wrong things—or too many things—our actions trip up our momentum.

Rather than doing everything and trying to grow in every direction, try focusing on the specific outcome you desire. If you don't work toward the outcome you want, you mostly likely won't get it. Instead, you'll arrive at a place where, even though you've put in an enormous amount of "sweat equity," your life still isn't what you want it to be. You'll either still be running around like a chicken without a head, as busy as ever because your business is still totally dependent on your constant presence, or you'll end up burned out, sitting all alone on a pile of money, wondering what to do with yourself because you haven't taken the time to sustain lasting personal relationships and meaningful outside pursuits.

Again, as Stephen Covey once said, "You want to begin with the end in mind."

It's almost become a cliché these days to say, "Work smarter, not harder." But there's a reason it's a cliché; working smarter instead of just working harder is a crucial element of the IDEAL Business. It's not that my philosophy is about avoiding hard work or believing in the "make money in your pajamas" promise. It's about *working from a strategic place*. A focused strategy allows you to make every minute of your work count, create higher quality results from your efforts, and gain the time to enjoy a rich personal life, all while you continue to build toward an outcome that provides the kind of lifestyle you'd like for yourself and your loved ones.

If you're anything like me, you became (or desire to become) an entrepreneur because you wanted to control your own destiny. Unfortunately, it's common to limit those ambitions to the context of business. Outside of our businesses, we often fail to pursue that kind of control in the outcomes we experience. Like the client I wrote about at the beginning of this chapter, we allow our work to creep in and steal from other important areas of our lives. All my client had to do to make sure his family time was enjoyable for all concerned was to turn off his phone—a simple way of maintaining control of his personal life for a few hours.

For some reason, as entrepreneurs we forget that we *do* control all the pieces of our lives. We know, of course, that we must control all the pieces of our businesses to make them grow and succeed. But we aren't always so intentional about our lives outside of business, and that ends up taking a toll. It may be fun to engage in wishful thinking and believe that everything will magically be okay at some unknown date in the future, but that attitude of denial becomes destructive over time.

Our goal, as entrepreneurs and business leaders is to work on making life—all of life—as enjoyable and healthy and strong as we can *now*.

## It's All in Your Head

One of the biggest secrets to building a successful life and business is believing we're actually capable of doing it. And to be fair to entrepreneurs, sometimes that's a heavy lift.

Most people go to work for other folks and depend on them to advance their careers. If that progression doesn't happen, they go to work for somebody else who will help them climb the ladder. Entrepreneurs don't have other people to help them up the ladder. They must climb it all by themselves. As a matter of fact, there *is* no ladder unless the entrepreneur makes one of their own (or subcontracts to get the job done)!

This means an entrepreneur's mind-set is all-important. When we have the right attitudes in place, our success literally has no ceiling. When our thinking is either negative or unfocused, however, it's hard to get anything off the floor. We all know that person who repeatedly makes the same mistake. We say to ourselves, "There goes old Bob again, screwing up a perfect thing as only Bob can do." The problem is "old Bob" never seems to catch on to his self-defeating behavior. Next time around, he's failing himself in the exact same way, oblivious to his own pattern.

For example, maybe you have a friend who consistently dates the same personality type. Every time it's a disaster because this type is completely wrong for your friend. Yet after he ends one relationship, he goes right ahead and starts a new one with the very same personality type. Or, maybe you know someone who constantly asks to borrow money from you because she overspends every month. She always says she's going to get her budget together, but then next month she calls up asking for another small loan.

According to a great deal of research, the reason we repeatedly make the same mistakes is because we're too preoccupied with them in our daily lives. That obsession bugs the neurons in our subconscious brain and motivates it to try and "help" us solve the recurring problem. I put *help* in quotes because, unfortunately, the brain's solution just makes things worse. It motivates us to commit the error all over again so it can study the process, and all that does is continue the problematic loop!

The real solution—and again, this is according to the scientists—is to stop dwelling on the past, because that just makes your brain want to recreate everything you're trying to escape. Instead, focus on what you want to do—what you're *going to do.*

That's why I say, "It's all in your head." We have a choice in our lives. We can either look forward and keep planning on how to bring more prosperity and happiness into our lives, or we can just keep going around in circles, reliving unproductive, self-destructive or limiting patterns that keep us stuck—or worse, push us backwards. We have the power; we just need to put it to work for us.

## IDEAL BUSINESS RULE #4: IF YOU DON'T THINK YOU CAN DO IT, YOU WON'T.

For more than two decades I've been studying the direct link between our thoughts and the reality we create for ourselves, and I'm here to tell you there is much truth behind this idea. One of my favorite books on this subject is *As a Man Thinketh* by James Allen, one of the pioneers in the inspirational thought movement. Even though the book is more than a century old, the Bible verse it's based on, "As a man thinketh in his heart, so is he" (Proverbs 23:7), articulates a truth that will always be relevant to our lives. You don't have to be a religious person to understand that. If you haven't already done so, I highly encourage you to read *As a Man Thinketh* and examine your own thought processes and how they impact your business and life.

Understanding precedes change. Before we can make a positive change in our results, we must first understand what controls our results. When we really begin to understand how our minds work—and to what extent our thoughts control our outcomes—we can unlock great transformations in every aspect of our lives. This process of change and growth will undoubtedly force you out of your comfort zone, but that's the point. We all need to break out of our individual mental boxes so we can grow beyond where we are now.

## Thinking Makes It So

Here's a little more science to help you understand the power of mind-set. Psychologist Martin Seligman, author of *Learned Optimism*, has found that when things go wrong, pessimists make it personal. Believing that negative results are inevitable, pessimists aren't inclined to even try to make things better. For example, when they mess up a presentation, they chalk it up to their own lack of talent as a public speaker. They think it's useless to try and improve themselves, so they never get better; they continue to fail at the task.

Positive thinking can be a way out of your box and a key to your success in all things. Let's consider how the example of the person whose presentation bombed might be different if that person were an optimist. As a positive-minded person, that person would believe improvement is always possible, and he would practice to ensure improvement before the next presentation.

Again, science backs up the idea that positive thinking can affect outcomes. Here are the results of two business-related studies cited in *Psychology Today*:

- Economists who surveyed over one thousand American CEOs found that more than 80 percent were found to be "very optimistic."
- In a study of salespeople over a two-year period, the optimists outsold the pessimists by 37 percent.

This isn't to say we should view life as a family-friendly, Disney movie where happy endings are guaranteed. We know that's not true. Just as we need optimism to see possibilities, we need realistic thinking to recognize threats and problems and tackle them before they spin out of control. But, ultimately, if you don't allow yourself to see light at the end of a tunnel, it may be almost impossible to find your way out of a dark spot.

## Looking beyond the Obvious

My career started out in the fitness business, which means I know how important regular exercise is to healthy muscles. Without it, your muscles atrophy. Your mind is no different. If you don't exercise your mental muscles, if you don't work to think beyond your normal patterns, you miss important opportunities to innovate and excel.

For example, one of the worst traps you can walk into is simply duplicating what everyone else in your industry is doing. You structure your company like they do, you market your products and services like they do, and you know what? Everybody looks at you as just another version of what's already out there—only an inferior version because the rest of your competitors were doing it all first.

How does that help you stand out? It doesn't.

In contrast, one of the great things you can do is look outside your industry and see how someone else is achieving great things with a business, then use those techniques—if they fit—in your business.

For example, Robert Palmer began his mortgage business in Florida right after the real estate crash of 2007, possibly the worst time in recorded history to do so. And speaking of history, up until that time, most mortgage brokers had worked with real estate agents to get their clients' business through referrals. Palmer, however, applied proven direct marketing tactics to go right after home buyers themselves to loan them money. The result was, his company, RP Funding, became a fast and huge success because he made himself a Category of One. (I'll go into more detail about this later in Chapter 6.)

Perception is reality. So much depends on how you look at things. When you change your point of view and examine a situation from another angle, you see things you might have missed, which could provide you with valuable insight into that situation that you otherwise might never have obtained. When you're building the IDEAL Business, it's important to open your mind to all your possibilities and not limit yourself to the tried-and-true business models that your competition is using.

My next rule represents one of the most important lessons I learned while developing an IDEAL mind-set, and it's this:

## IDEAL BUSINESS RULE #5: JUST BECAUSE YOU DON'T SEE IT DOESN'T MEAN IT ISN'T THERE.

I want to share with you a simple illustration of this concept of seeing the invisible. Now, I'm sure you're familiar with this world-renowned corporate logo:

There's something particularly brilliant about the design of this logo that most people don't even realize and it's this: There is an arrow deliberately created within the space between the "E" and the "x." Now, once you realize it's there, you don't forget about it. You spot it every time. But if you don't know it's there, you don't think it exists. Why would you?

Now, here's another logo that does something similar:

Most people only see the image in the top left corner of the Goodwill logo as part of a smiling face. But, if you give it a closer look, you'll see it also forms the stylized "g" from the Goodwill font.

Now, in both cases, millions of people look at those logos every day and have no idea the arrow or the smiling "g" exist. But if you pressed them to look at these logos in a different way, they'd see them in a flash.

"Okay," you might be saying. "What does this have to do with the IDEAL mind-set?"

I'll tell you. We often don't see alternative ways of doing business because we don't allow ourselves to look beyond the status quo. We accept the standard attitudes and traditional approaches without looking past them toward other solutions that could improve our entrepreneurial lives in all areas. However, if we don't consciously seek out opportunities to do things differently in our businesses or our lives, we're never going to see them— which means there's no way we're ever going to try them. How can we? We have no idea what they are!

Sometimes it's necessary to believe in what's invisible. We must trust that we will see the paths to creating the life we want for ourselves—and believe in our capabilities to successfully travel those paths. If we don't think that we can achieve great things, we won't achieve them. If we don't believe we can create the IDEAL Life and the IDEAL Business for ourselves, we won't make the attempt; we will accept our self-made limitations and stay in the box that we've placed ourselves in.

We do have control over our outcomes, but we must dedicate ourselves to pursuing them. One of my favorite quotes from George Bernard Shaw puts it this way:

*People are always blaming their circumstances for what they are. I don't believe in circumstances. The people who get on in this world are the people who get up and look for the circumstances they want, and if they can't find them, make them.*

To that, I offer a big "Amen."

I'd like to wrap up this section by talking for a moment about how my mind-set toward adversity has changed over time. I'll open with the disclaimer that I've not experienced a real tragedy at this point in my own personal life, so what I'm referring to as adversity here is really a bump in the road. An obstacle. I've hit *plenty* of those. In fact, I can think back to various points in my own professional life where I encountered an obstacle and, at times, felt like a failure. Maybe you can relate to my story.

When I graduated from college, I applied for more than sixty graduate assistant or volunteer assistant coaching opportunities. I didn't get a single interview. At the time, I felt like a failure.

Ultimately, not having an assistant position left me available to take the position as the head baseball coach and head strength coach at my alma mater—a position that provided me opportunities to learn and grow in a way that being a graduate assistant might never have.

After building that program from perennial loser to national competitor, I was forced to resign. My self-image was crushed. Up to that point, being a college coach had been my identity. Suddenly, I had to shift and take a different route professionally. I ended up moving to Lexington, Kentucky, (where I met my wife, Holly), and I became an entrepreneur and built a number of businesses.

About a decade later, I hit a wall professionally and decided to make a change. This time it was my choice and decision to move away from something I built, but in some ways, that made the change feel even more challenging. My decision impacted a lot of other people, including my family, employees, clients, and franchisees.

Fast forward a couple of years, and I'm having considerably more impact than the previous organization ever had, and I'm having far more fun doing it. Time and time again, my experience has been that something better was just on the other side of a challenge. Greater success was the reward for moving past an obstacle.

I'd suspect the same holds true for you.

I think in business, challenges are simply presented to weed out those who aren't truly suited to be business owners. Great things shouldn't come easily. If they did, they'd simply be ordinary. Rather, obstacles, adversity, and challenges are opportunities to reveal the greatness that lies within you. They're the precursor to something that will likely be even better than your past or present situation. With that in mind, embrace the things that seem like challenges today; they are opportunities for a better tomorrow.

In the next chapter, we're going to move from the theoretical to the practical with some hands-on advice on building your IDEAL Business. Specifically, we'll look at what needs to go into its foundation so you can build the kind of success you want.

# CHAPTER 3

# THE IDEAL FOUNDATION

I worked at a state university for more than seven years. The standard annual pay increase for most who worked there was three percent. You got a raise, basically, for showing up to work. As long as you didn't screw up, you could look forward to that bump in salary every year like clockwork. Not only that, but you got two weeks of paid vacation, paid sick days, good health insurance, and your hours were fixed (9:00 a.m. to around 4:30 p.m.). You could go home at night, completely disconnect from your job, and enjoy the evening as you saw fit.

Pretty good deal, right?

If you're an entrepreneur (or want to be one), that "good deal" is okay, and maybe it's a good enough place to be while you turn a side hustle into a profitable business. But most people who decide to be entrepreneurs do so because we want more than the salaried life offers. We want to be in charge of our income, our hours, and our lives.

However, do you truly feel in charge? Or do you feel like your business is running you?

I consult with a lot of entrepreneurs, and I get to see close-up how much they do and how much time they put in. Their commitment is total. I also see how many people they help with their products and services, as well as how they impact their communities as business owners.

What they earn in return is often, well, mortifying. They're not making the money they should. They're not able to take vacations or days off. They carry work in their head 24/7. Many don't have 401ks or IRAs or any of the other normal employee perks, even though *they're the bosses.* That's why many of them come to me: They want help making some tweaks to turn things around.

When I start digging in, I discover how hard that assignment is going to be. Because, believe it or not, they never took the time to design their businesses with those positive goals in mind.

We entrepreneurs take more risks than salaried employees. We take on much more responsibility. We make a significant, positive impact in the marketplace and in our communities by contributing to the economy, creating jobs, and adding value to an area. So why shouldn't we realize bigger rewards than the average employee? Doesn't it sound like we deserve them?

Here's where business is a whole lot like life: Just because you deserve something doesn't mean you're going to get it. That's why you must be proactive about making sure you get those rewards. If you want bigger rewards (and more income), you must be intentional about the choices you make as you create and structure your business.

Personal choice is an important ongoing theme you'll see repeated as we get into the nuts and bolts of creating the IDEAL Business. It all starts here. In this chapter we'll look at four basic principles you need to put into place so you can build the strongest and most fruitful foundation for future growth, success, and the best work-life balance. These principles apply whether you're starting a new business or, if like me, you'd like to make the shift in your current business to make it IDEAL.

Stick to these basics and you'll set yourself up for great, positive results in the years to come.

## *IDEAL Principle 1: It All Starts with You*

Here's what I consider to be a shocking fact: On every strategic business planning tool I've ever seen, personal objectives are never made a part of the discussion.

Isn't that a little strange? I don't mean to disparage these planning tools; I've certainly learned a lot from them. But they are normally designed for big businesses with corporate structures rather than the entrepreneurial start-up. Often, these kinds of planning tools are also typically the only ones we can find online. Personal goals don't have a place in these corporate planning tools so our individual goals aren't given a chance to be part of the mix.

If that's the model or the kind of planning tool you started with, the IDEAL Business approach will fill that gap. We're going to flip that picture and start the planning process with personal priorities rather than professional ones. Right now, I want you to write down the three things that are most important to you personally in terms of what you want out of your life—your true passions. The choices are up to you, of course, but here are a few items to spark ideas for the kinds of things that could end up on your list:

- Work
- Family
- Friends
- Faith
- Travel
- Personal Fitness
- Exciting Experiences
- Personal Growth
- Charity

Now, let's take a closer look at the three passions you picked.

Go back and look through your bank account records for the past three months. Analyze how much of your financial resources you allocated to the three things you picked. For example, if you traveled, how much did you spend on a trip?

Not every one of the three passions you chose will have a financial component; for example, if you're a *Game of Thrones* fanatic, the only cost is your HBO subscription. That is, of course, unless you're into buying swords, helmets, and stuffed dragons. Now, *that* could cost you some money. The point is, you can't judge every item strictly by how much you spend on them, which is why I'd like you to do a second exercise with your list of three biggest passions. Calculate how much time you've spent doing those three activities in the past month. If something is truly vital to the enjoyment of your life, there should be an ample investment of your time. If that time component isn't there—for example, if you say family is important to you and you found you only spent a few hours on family activities in the past thirty days—the lack of time indicates a problem with your priorities.

The purpose of all this calculation is to determine not only your life passions, but how much time and money you're able to commit to them. If that commitment is lacking, if you're not able to enjoy your passions, then it's time make fulfilling them a part of your business strategy. In other words, make the business work for you, not the other way around.

You may even be lucky enough to be able to make your passions an integral part of your business. I always had a passion for personal fitness, and that's the field where I found entrepreneurial success.

Which brings me to my next rule…

## IDEAL BUSINESS RULE #6: DO WHAT YOU LOVE, AND YOU'LL NEVER HATE GOING TO WORK.

Makes sense, right?

## *IDEAL Principle 2: Play to Your Strengths, Understand Your Values*

In addition to identifying your passions, I want you to take some time to identify your strongest talents, skills, and traits. Your business should reflect what's best about you and what excites you. You don't want to base it on your weak points or what you hate doing.

As you consider your talents, skills, and positive traits, think about what people compliment you on. Consider the reasons people hire you or come to your facility or office. We'll talk more about this when we talk about branding, but for now, identify the things about you that have already brought you some degree of success and write them down.

If you're still not sure about what your specific strengths might be, send an email to five different people and say, "What do you think are my top three strengths?" They'll answer with suggestions that will get your brain working in the right direction.

Of course, even though you've identified those strengths, you need to know that running a business makes you deal with areas that don't involve your strengths—areas that require abilities you don't possess or don't care about. The trick is to structure your business in such a way that you minimize your involvement in those areas and maximize your involvement in roles in which you excel.

For example, you may hate the selling part of your business, but that's certainly a crucial part of any profit-oriented operation. You may need to put in place a strong salesperson who can do the heavy lifting in that area. Or to use another example, you may stink at accounting. If so, you need to find a resource that can help you make your numbers add up.

It's all about playing to your strengths and passions. For those tasks that simply aren't in your wheelhouse, you want to delegate and elevate. Find people whom you trust to handle the parts of the business you want to avoid and, at the same time, get yourself to a position where you feel like you don't have to get your hands dirty with them. Instead, just keep a close eye on those who are taking care of those tasks to ensure you're still getting the results you expect or want.

In addition to your strengths, at this juncture you also want to identify and list your core values. Obviously, you want to make sure your business doesn't violate your values. For example, family, integrity, and my responsibility to coach others to maximize their potential are some of my big core values. Those are some of the values I want to be known for in my work.

Why is it important to identify your core values? Because these values become the filter for all your decisions. Either a choice fits with those values or it doesn't. If a business opportunity takes me away from my family for a month or two at a time, I won't commit to it. It violates one of my core values and I don't want to lose that family connection just for a few more dollars.

It's hard for us to reach our potential as business owners unless we play to our strengths and stick to our core values. It's also hard for us to feel fulfilled personally if we are continually forced to compromise our belief systems. That's why this principle of playing to your strengths and understanding your values is foundational to building a company you'll enjoy running and will feel proud of for a very long time.

### IDEAL Principle 3: Determine What Success Looks Like to You

When I ask the question, "What does success look like to you?" I'm not just talking about how big your company becomes or how high your annual revenues might go. I'm talking about your own long-term goals. I'm talking about answering the most important question of your strategic process: *Why did you start a business in the first place?*

Why did you assume all this risk and responsibility? Why did you decide to take on the necessary sacrifices involved with entrepreneurship to go out on your own? Why didn't you just take the easy way out and go work for some big company?

Here are some common answers I hear from entrepreneurs:

- "I want to build a business that genuinely helps a lot of people."
- "I want to earn a certain level of income, and this is the only way I can do it."
- "I want to be able to control my own destiny, not be at the mercy of a big corporate bureaucracy."

Whatever your answer is, it must be strong enough to sustain you through the grind of keeping your business running. There will be days when it will seem like too much. However, if you keep why you're doing this top-of-mind, it helps see you through the difficulties and keeps you on track. Think of your *why* as the destination for your own mental GPS system. If you don't have an end point programmed, your GPS can't map out a path for you. But when you know where you want to go, you can figure out a path to get there.

What is your end goal—your purpose for being in business? Once you've identified your reason(s), write out a short and impactful mission statement for both yourself and your business. In other words, figure out what you ultimately want out of your business and what you want to get out of it for yourself.

Once you have those big goals in your head, it's time to figure out how you reach them. That will require some reverse engineering through setting some short-term process goals. Here's a quick example of what a process goal is all about: Let's say, as a personal trainer, I had a client who wanted to lose twenty pounds in ten weeks. How would I help this person do that? We'd set weekly targets of losing just two pounds each week and develop a plan to accomplish that. Then, on a weekly basis we'd check in to see how she was progressing and amend the plan if needed.

It's important to create those same kinds of objectives for yourself in your entrepreneurial role. Process goals help you incrementally close in on your larger business and personal goals. Take some time and think through a few. I suggest you use the proven SMART system when setting these types of goals. SMART is an acronym that stands for the following:

- **S**pecific
- **M**easurable
- **A**chievable
- **R**elevant
- **T**ime-bound (i.e. each goal has a deadline or series of deadlines for being met)

Once you establish where you want to go, reverse engineer your goals. Determine exactly how you're going to make your goals a reality. It's great to say you want to expand your square footage by 50 percent, but that goal does you no good unless you specifically state *how* you're going to fund the expansion.

If you break process goals into smaller actionable pieces, you'll be amazed at what you can achieve. One business owner who consulted with me was seriously overworking himself. A major part of the problem was he didn't believe he could change the situation. I had him cut his workload on just two days of the week. We started by just ending his workday an hour earlier than he had previously been stopping. Once that seemed manageable, we shortened it by one more hour. He began handing off some simple tasks that he'd traditionally just defaulted to doing. He became more efficient because he was no longer spreading his tasks out in a longer day, and he began to think, *"This is possible.*

*I can do more to get myself out from under this constant stress."*
Small wins contribute heavily to big victories, and when you
make a little bit of progress each day, you end up hitting a big
target relatively quickly.

### IDEAL Principle 4: Create a Culture of Production

One of my favorite words is producer. To build your IDEAL
Business and to meet its goals, *you* must produce; nobody's going
to do it for you. On the client or customer side, it's your job to
produce the results they're seeking, the high-level experience that
keeps them coming back, and the products they want to buy.

That's the challenge every entrepreneur faces. I know you work
hard to deliver to your clients or patients, but I'm going to offer
one more challenge for you: Work hard for *yourself* by producing
the necessary business revenue and growth that will allow you to
not only prosper but to also provide both your security and your
freedom.

Your first step toward that is to create a culture of production
where *you're keeping score*. Metrics must be involved in what
you're doing so you can determine if you're making the kind of
progress you want to make. Within those metrics, targets must be
set so you can judge whether you're getting the essential things
done. Either you achieve your numbers or you don't. It makes
things simple.

The metrics you choose to measure will depend on what your
specific business is all about. Here are a few common categories
where keeping score can be crucial:

- Number of clients/customers/patients per day
- Revenues earned per day
- Number of referrals received per week
- Number of sales calls successfully completed per day
- Number of conversions of those sales calls

You can wait and calculate your daily averages at the end of the month if you want, but it's good to track the most important numbers of your business sooner rather than later so you can take steps to fix any trends that might be going in the wrong direction.

Apply some *life* metrics to your situation too. Are you taking enough vacation days so you don't get burnt out? Are you spending enough personal hours either with family or doing something you love that's not about work?

Keeping score is critical to understanding how well you are (or aren't) doing. Imagine an NFL season where nobody kept track of touchdowns, field goals, etc. Teams wouldn't be ranked, standings wouldn't exist, and stats wouldn't matter. Fans would get bored, teams wouldn't be motivated, and the whole league would fall apart. Keeping score keeps everybody on their toes— including you and your employees. Good metrics ensure that you stay productive.

One final note: One of the best ways to create a culture of production and fulfill your role as a producer is to surround yourself with achievers. This goes for your friends, your employees, and your business associates. Having motivated people in your circle helps motivate you. They inspire you with their accomplishments, and their positive can-do attitudes bring a lot of good energy into your life. This is such an important thing to remember that it's worth a rule of its own:

### IDEAL BUSINESS RULE #7: YOU DO BETTER WHEN THE PEOPLE AROUND YOU WANT TO DO BETTER.

Plato said, *"The beginning is the hardest part of the work."* I think it's also the most important. Putting these four basic principles to work in your business will ensure that success will look the way you want it to. That's as ideal a situation as you can imagine!

# CHAPTER 4

# GUARDRAILS

Let's talk about guardrails. No, this isn't going to be a lecture on highway safety. I want to talk instead about theoretical guardrails. Confused? It really isn't that complicated. Read on and you'll see what I'm getting at.

So far in this book, I've shared a lot of ideas that I believe can help any entrepreneur focus on building a prosperous and satisfying life. But I know a few of you may be thinking: *General principles aren't practical. I have to do what works for my business, and that's a very day-to-day thing. I can't be guided by theoretical concepts; I have to deal with reality.*

It may be true that you need to make many different decisions every day at your business. These decisions are mostly operational and revolve around how to get the best results for your bottom line. I get that. I also get that your business may be different from mine, but where your business and mine (and every other business out there) line up is the fact that the different choices we make every day *are informed by the specific vision we have about what we want our businesses to be.* The choices we make eventually add up to create a very specific outcome.

It's not unlike driving a car. Sometimes you've got to step on the gas; sometimes you've got to hit the brakes. Sometimes you're on a big open freeway with the car on cruise control, and other times you're trapped in traffic, stopping and starting every few seconds. Sometimes you've got a smooth ride, and other times your car suddenly breaks down and you end up on the shoulder, calling for help. And sometimes you make a wrong turn and you have no idea where you are!

On almost every highway these days, you're going to find guardrails to the side—especially around sharp curves and on bridges. Those guardrails are there, of course, to keep you from flying off the road if you should lose control of your car. Well, I'd like you to think of your own ambitions for your life and your business as being like those guardrails. If you keep them in place and remind yourself of their importance, you'll keep your business—and your life—straight on course for success.

Before I go further, I want to give some credit to my friend and entrepreneur extraordinaire John Berardi who introduced me to the idea of guardrails. I have to thank him for allowing me to borrow the term; I think it's a great metaphor for how you can keep yourself on track toward your goals.

Guardrails represent your rules of engagement. When you keep those rules in mind, it forces you to take a few steps back from those constant and sometimes overwhelming day-to-day decisions and, instead, consider them within the context of your big picture objectives (and how you want to attain them). That kind of perspective motivates you to ask yourself questions like: *What matters to me the most in this situation? What will advance this business—and what might make it regress? How does this decision affect my overall quality of life?* Suddenly you start steering yourself toward your own personal happiness.

Without those guardrails in place, however, you end up *reacting* instead of *acting*. You let outside circumstances—instead of your heart and mind—dictate what you do. Yes, life is always a delicate balance between what you want and what the world says you can have. But don't you want to at least control as much of your destiny as you can?

Now, you've probably never thought of guardrails as being magical, but the kind I'm talking about in this chapter are, at least to me. Yet, when I communicate this basic idea of establishing rules of engagement, the reaction of some entrepreneurs is, "Well, if I try to enforce these guardrails, if I stick to these rules on an ongoing basis, that's going to limit my success." They see these guardrails as hindering their happiness, not enabling it.

I've found the exact opposite to be true. Parameters force you to be more creative, which, in turn, creates more opportunity. Your guardrails put you in solution mode. You end up pushing yourself a little harder to seek a path that takes you to the outcome you seek, rather than settling for a quick and dirty way out that compromises your long-term plan. With guardrails, you learn to adapt and bring new ideas into your business instead of just doing what you've always been doing. Or worse, playing follow-the-leader with a competitor. They also help immensely with my next rule:

## IDEAL BUSINESS RULE #8: MAKE THINGS HAPPEN; DON'T LET THINGS HAPPEN TO YOU.

Now, let's talk about the danger of not abiding by this particular guardrail:

### The Danger of Drift

As I said, your guardrails keep you on the road toward the destination you have in mind. Without them...

You drift. And that, to me, is an entrepreneur's worst-case scenario.

Michael Hyatt talks about the danger of drifting in his best-selling book *Living Forward*. Drifting is when you just wake up and go through the motions of what you think you're supposed to be doing. You act like an employee instead of a business owner, and that's not why any of us decided to become an entrepreneur. If you remember the old Dunkin' Donuts commercial where the guy in the DD uniform leaves in the morning saying, "Time to make the donuts," then comes back at night and says, "I made the donuts"—and he does this again and again. Well, that's just what can happen when you don't make conscious choices about your life and your business. You just allow things to take their own course, trusting in magic or fate to take you to your desired income rather than putting in the effort to get there yourself.

How unfulfilling is that? You're still taking on a giant chunk of responsibility by running your own business, and you're still putting in an enormous amount of time to make it work. But at the end of the day, all that time and all those headaches just add up to you treading water—and while you're treading water, the current might just take you who-knows-where.

Drifting is sometimes just the result of starting out life with lowered expectations. Maybe, like me, you're from a small, economically-depressed town where the attitude was "Hey, if you can get a job, you're in pretty good shape!" No need to think much beyond that. Even though you went ahead and started your own business, you still might have put a low ceiling on what you could achieve with that business.

Or maybe other people have told you there are limits to how high you can climb. It happens. Usually that kind of message comes from people who are highly insecure about their own self-worth. Most don't mean to be malicious when they tell you that you can't do something; they just can't see how it can be done. They have no experience with the level of success you're aiming at. Often, they think they're protecting you. And sometimes they want to keep you in their orbit. They don't want you to reach for the stars, because if you do, that might disrupt their own comfort zone by challenging them to do more with their own lives.

Whatever the reason, remember this: It's up to you—and only

you—to decide what you want. That means you get to decide whom you'll work with, how you're going to work, when you're going to work, and how you're going to structure things in your business—and in your life.

You do all that by putting your own personal guardrails in place and keeping them in mind when you're making choices, both big and small.

## The Guidance of Guardrails

Let me go back to the man I mentioned earlier, the man who introduced me to the concept of guardrails, John Berardi. John is the co-founder of Precision Nutrition, the world's largest online nutrition coaching and professional education company, so he's no slouch when it comes to entrepreneurial effort. That's why it was a little bit of a surprise when he shared one of his own personal guardrails with me. He said, "Look, I only want to work Monday through Thursday, seven hours a day."

Pretty hardcore, right? But he does his best to stick to it.

Now, is this always going to work out for him? No. There will undoubtedly be a weekend event he wants to attend or a Friday business commitment he just can't get out of. That happens. But that schedule, that Monday-through-Thursday, seven-hours-a-day guardrail is *what guides him*. Those are the parameters he works within. He's got at least four good reasons for them too (because that's the number of kids he has, and he wants to spend Fridays with them). Often he'll just take the kids out of school that day so he can make that happen. Too bad he wasn't *my* dad, because that would have been fine with me!

Another one of his guardrails was to build a world-class education program without having to travel. That desire inspired a very unconventional outcome that produced amazing results: His business doesn't have a corporate office. It used to, but nobody actually showed up there to work. They all communicated with each other virtually, so there was no need for them to physically be in the same room. Even without a corporate office, they managed to build an amazingly successful program. That guardrail of not having to travel didn't limit John's aspirations or the company's possibilities. No, it energized them.

When you say something like, "Hey, I'm going to work four days a week and try to limit myself to seven hours a day," then suddenly you've put yourself in a position where you must say "No" to a ton of the trivial things that occupy most people's days. You don't have time for bureaucracy. You don't have time to chase your own tail. You only have time to attend to what's necessary and not much else. Perhaps that's all the time you need.

Now, this isn't to say that I haven't gotten a business email from John on a Saturday. Or a call on a Thursday night. That happens. But I'm sure when he finds himself doing too much of that kind of thing when it's supposed to be his downtime, he needs to course correct.

John is not a guy who wants to drift.

As for me? Here are a few of my guardrails:

First of all, I don't want to be gone more than two full days at a time for anything unless I've got some family with me, either my wife or both my wife and kids. So when somebody asks me, "Hey, wouldn't you love to go to China for a speaking engagement?" I don't think about it too long. Actually, I don't think about it at all; I just turn it down. The conversation is over.

Another important guardrail? The ability to work at home. I don't like to waste time commuting. I'm more comfortable in my own house and function better there, anyway. So why leave? That's why I do as much from home as possible.

A couple of years ago, I put a huge temporary guardrail in place, a guardrail so big it scared me a little. That was when I decided to coach both of my boys' baseball teams. If you've been involved in youth sports, you know what kind of time commitment coaching one team demands, let alone two teams. Every game and practice from late March until mid-July that year? Those were built into my calendar—and everything else I did during that time was scheduled around them.

Even that brutal guardrail didn't impact my ability to grow my business. I really believe that, in many cases, it facilitated efficiency and productivity. As I said earlier, boundaries force you to seek creative solutions that you might never have thought of otherwise. You try them out, and some of those new solutions become vital parts of your business approach because they save you time, provide quicker results, and/or make your life easier. That last point alone is enough for me.

Before you move on to the next chapter, I encourage you to think about the guardrails you want—or need—in your business and life. Here are a few questions to help you set up your guardrails:

1. What should be on your professional *not to-do* list?
2. What are the 20 percent of things that happen in your business that you should be spending the majority of your time?
3. What should you be doing less of, either because you don't enjoy it or because it's not the best use of your time for the success of the business?

# CHAPTER 5

# IDEAL LEADERSHIP

Leadership. You can't avoid it. No entrepreneur can. That's because, ultimately, it's your business (or businesses). You're steering the ship, you're choosing the course, and you're making the final calls. That's an awesome responsibility. You're the ultimate decision-maker, and those decisions can't help but have a huge impact on not only your success, but the success of the people who work for you.

In the previous chapter, I talked about the kinds of personal guardrails that keep you from flying off the road. When you want to create certain boundaries in your life, these guardrails can be invaluable. However, your entrepreneurial journey is about more than staying on the road, of course. It's about putting yourself on the right road—the road to success—so you can achieve the best outcome for you, your team, and your customers or patients.

Most of us, however, are ill-prepared for the kind of leadership role our businesses require. Instead, we get thrown into the deep end and are forced to find our way without much experience in or knowledge about how to effectively lead. That was certainly the case with me when I became a baseball coach at the tender age of twenty-three. I certainly didn't know what I was doing. I had to sort out for myself what worked and what didn't. I did that by watching how coaches I admired did their jobs. I did it by reading books written by respected leadership experts like John Maxwell. Most importantly, I learned by *doing*, every single day on the field.

I guess I picked up the right leadership lessons because I believe I did right by my baseball team. And after that, I did right by my businesses. I had integrated some core leadership principles into my life. These core principles never let me down. Over the years, I've broken them down into seven rules that have served me well. Yes, that's right; you get seven rules in one single chapter.

Now, most of these rules may seem like common sense, but it's surprising how *un*common common sense can be. That's why I try to keep the following "Magnificent Seven" top-of-mind in my own leadership challenges, and I hope you will as well. Together, they reflect a unified philosophy about leadership that I continue to hold to this day, which I'll share at the close of this chapter.

### Rule of Leadership #1: The Golden Rule Still Works

This rule is short and sweet, and it comes down to this: Treat people the way you'd want to be treated.

We don't really exist in an era anymore where we can bully great work out of people. And I think that's a good thing. It's hard for folks who are scared and shaking, wondering what abuse the boss is going to heap on them, to really function at a high level. They're afraid to take chances, even when they should. They're afraid to tell the person in charge bad news, even when they need to.

Bullying causes employees to always "color inside the lines." They rarely grow or innovate because doing something different brings the danger of doing something wrong. Your team doesn't feel encouraged to find new and better solutions; rather, they follow instructions down to the letter to ensure their survival.

Think about what motivated you to over-deliver over the years. Think about what kind of behavior by authority figures such as parents, teachers, and former bosses pushed you forward, instead of making you feel like you had to cower in a corner. I'm willing to bet a positive approach, backed up by a genuine interest in your success, gave you the confidence you needed to improve and grow to become the entrepreneur you are today.

## Rule of Leadership #2: Get Everybody Rowing Together

As I said, a leader sets the direction for an enterprise. The big problem comes when not everyone involved believes in or works toward that direction.

You've probably seen the ancient galley ships in old movies like *Ben Hur*, the massive ones used by the Romans and the Greeks that had as many as a hundred men in the lower deck rowing at once to propel them forward. A hundred guys rowing at once, of course, provides immense power and speed to any sea-worthy vessel.

But imagine the difference in the speed of one of those ships if all those rowers decided not to row simultaneously. Or worse, some of them decided to row in the opposite direction. That's going to make for a slow and not-so-satisfying journey.

That metaphor applies to your business. When you and your people all believe in and work toward the same goals, you've got a much greater chance of achieving them because you're all "rowing in unison." That unison creates a directed force that outstrips the competition with ease.

I learned this truth when I was a baseball coach. It was more than a matter of all of us wanting to make it to the collegiate World Series; it was also all of us *believing in the process that would get us there.* The majority of my players bought into the systems I put in place, and that fact alone helped us surge past a lot of better-funded teams with higher-profile recruits.

That's why it's important for you as a business leader to explain to your people not only *what* goal you're trying to reach, but the *how* and *why* behind that goal. The more your team understands your approach and the reasons behind it, the more likely they will end up reaching their potential and enjoying their role on the team. When everyone is "rowing" together, you're going to speed toward your destination.

As the leader, you must communicate your vision clearly and on a regular basis. If someone balks at it, talk with them about their concerns. Maybe they have a point, and maybe you need to adjust your thinking based on what they say. Or, it might be they misunderstand your intentions. Whatever the case, clear the air and make sure everyone is moving in the same direction.

A shared vision is a powerful lever for success.

## Rule of Leadership #3: Leverage Your People's Strengths

Back in 2001, business consultant Jim Collins wrote the massive bestseller, *Good to Great: Why Some Companies Make the Leap... and Others Don't.* The book resonated with me at the time and still does to this day. Collins' main point was this: Businesses succeed through the simple act of hiring the right people, putting them in the right jobs—and never letting go of that disciplined approach.

When your people come in with an attitude of achievement and are allowed to play to their strengths within your organization, they stay motivated and tend to excel in their performance. And that, of course, benefits everyone within your business. In my own experience, I've found that entrepreneurs who stick to that philosophy end up smelling like roses, even after they've gone through some times that stunk on ice.

Collins uses, as an example, David Maxwell, who became CEO of Fannie Mae in 1981. At that time, the company was losing a million dollars a day, and the board wanted to know exactly what Maxwell was going to do about it. Maxwell responded that they shouldn't be asking a "what" question, they should be asking a "who" question—as in who should make up the kind of management team that would get them out of this mess. Who had the strongest work ethics, the specific talents needed, and the drive needed to turn things around?

With that game plan, Maxwell examined his current management team. He told them what he required out of them to turn things around. Fourteen of the twenty-six execs ended up departing, and Maxwell replaced them with some of the best, smartest, and hardest-working executives in the world of finance. And only *then* did he turn his attention to the "what" question.

The result? At the end of Maxwell's CEO tenure, Fannie Mae was no longer losing a million a day. It was *earning* four million a day.

Does this law seem to contradict the previous one about having a shared vision? Yes and no. The idea here is that you can't follow through with the shared vision without having the right people to help you pursue that vision. With the right people, when your vision does need to evolve, you'll have a team that can help ensure your new direction's success.

As we all know, marketplaces change, economic conditions change, industries change, and that means your goals might have to change too. That's a lot easier to accomplish when you have smart and talented people in place. The right team members can help you adjust to changing conditions and maybe even see them coming before you do.

I first learned this rule of leadership as a baseball coach. It was a necessity. I not only had to get the right players on my team, I also had to figure out the roles to which they were most suited. Was a certain pitcher best as a starter or a reliever? Did a batter produce better batting in the third spot or the sixth? Was some guy better at catching balls in the infield or the outfield?

The process isn't that much different in the business world. If you put people in roles closely aligned with their unique talents, everybody's going to be better off. They'll be happier and more fulfilled, and because of that, they'll deliver a higher level of work.

**Rule of Leadership #4: Catch People Doing Something *Right***

My last rule sang the praises of hiring and supporting great employees who work hard to boost the performance of your business. In this rule, we're going to talk about what you can do to boost the performance of your employees.

I think you'll agree it's a whole lot more common for bosses to focus their energies on trying to catch their people doing something wrong. I prefer to catch them doing something *right*.

As a leader, I know I must accept this fact: When I hand off a responsibility or give a new role to a trusted employee, they're probably going to nail 90 to 95 percent of that assignment. Most of what they do for my business is going to be spot on. But that other 5 to 10 percent? They're going to mess that part up.

I've learned that there's no point in me getting upset about it. It's not like I'm perfect; I've been known to make a few mistakes here and there. We all do. It's part of being human. So I'm not going to judge an employee's overall performance by the small mistakes that fall within that 5 to 10 percent range. It's the price I pay for the nine out of ten things that they're going to do well that make my life easier.

However, I do see a lot of business owners who insist on shining a spotlight on that 5 or 10 percent that goes wrong. They look right past the fact that an employee is doing almost everything right and instead obsess on trying to catch their people doing things wrong. It's a negative, oppressive outlook and one I've been a victim of perpetuating.

I spent too many years as a baseball coach not really enjoying a win on the field. Most of the time, a victory was just a relief to me. During a game, in which we were leading, I would worry so much about all the ways we could screw it up. By the time the ninth inning was done so was I. I was so emotionally exhausted, I couldn't get as excited as I should have been about gaining a "W." Instead, I just felt lucky to get out alive!

I finally realized my attitude was not only harmful to me, but also to the rest of the team. If I can't fully celebrate a win, then my players are going to see it in my attitude and not be able to enjoy it as much either. With a little more experience under my belt, however, I was finally able to let go of what the team might have done wrong and embrace what they did right. I learned that the only way to reinforce confidence and create a culture of positive teamwork was to highlight our highs, not our lows.

That was a big turning point for me, and it can be for you too. When the business succeeds, make sure everyone feels good about that success—especially yourself!

## Rule of Leadership #5: Lift Up Your People, Lift Up Your Business

Part of the reason you became an entrepreneur was, undoubtedly, because you didn't want to limit yourself. By running your own business, there would be nobody above you to stop you from growing and becoming as great a business leader as you wanted to be. And yet many of us put that kind of ceiling on our own people's development.

We tell a new employee that we're paying them to do a particular job and that it's their responsibility to learn how to do that job. Then all we leave them with is a training manual or, worse, a list of their duties. If they've got anything on the ball, then they learn how to fulfill those duties, but not much else. Why? Because we don't coach them or educate them about how to do their job to the highest degree possible or even how to live up to our company's brand standards (more on those later).

True leadership isn't just about filling an open position and walking away from the person you hired. In my opinion, it's about helping to make those employees as good as they can possibly be by encouraging their talents and helping them to use those talents within the business.

In the fitness business, I would ask my clients, "What's your goal? Where do you want to get with your workouts?" I would then assess where they currently were and design a program to help them realize their physical fitness ambitions. I like to do the same with my employees. I believe if I really want to bring out the best in them, I need to invest in their growth and performance.

Does that sound like a ridiculous idea? Like some kind of make-believe fairy-tale business idea that can't work in the real world? If it does, let me talk briefly about another company very much associated with make-believe and fairy tales—but is also very much committed to fiscal success. That company is Disney, one of the companies I admire most in today's business world. Their corporate philosophy maintains that developing their "cast" (i.e., their workforce) is even more important than taking care of their guests. They know an amazing workforce can't help but create an amazing experience for Disney customers.

To quote the company's "Be My Guest" brochure detailing their customer service policies: "The magic of Disney's customer service has a quality that leads to superior organizational performance, building Guest satisfaction and increasing brand loyalty."

When you develop five people in their job roles, suddenly you have five times the reach with your brand than if you were doing it yourself. If you do it with ten people, you get ten times the reach. By taking the time to optimize your employees' talents, you grow your business from the inside out. They, in turn, are then going to be able to serve your customer base at an extremely high level.

## Rule of Leadership #6: Do as You Say

Parents are, in a way, the ultimate leaders. Their kids look up to them to learn how to behave and how to function in the world. It's a process that begins at birth; the impact a mom or dad has on that young impressionable mind is extraordinary. That's why parents must be careful. If they exhibit bad patterns in their own lives, the child is going to pick up on them and imitate them. For instance, if a parent swears like a truck driver around the house, that parent shouldn't be surprised when a toddler suddenly starts throwing around f-bombs like they were building blocks. The kid simply doesn't know better and assumes that's what they're expected to do.

In any leadership role, the same dynamic is in place, just on a smaller scale. An employer's behavior is much more powerful than their words. You can tell someone to keep his workspace neat and clean until you're blue in the face, but if your office looks like a tornado just blew through it and then came back for seconds, it's going to be hard for that employee to take you seriously. On a more meaningful level, if you aren't leading with integrity, if you aren't living the values you want your business to express, you can't blame your people for not doing it either.

Lead by example. Walk the walk. Demonstrate the qualities you want your people to display and they'll pick up on them. You'll be amazed at what a standard you can set for your entire business just by keeping to that standard yourself.

## Rule of Leadership #7: Employees Are People Too!

A little later in this book, I'm going to talk about how to develop your customer niche in such a way that you identify your most likely buyers and, just as importantly, understand who they are and what they want from you. In other words, you don't just view those who patronize your business as a bunch of dollar signs; you view them as *people* with the same kinds of concerns, aspirations and needs as you.

Well, I'm a big believer in viewing those who work for us as people too. After all, they don't exist in a vacuum, miraculously appearing at work and just as mysteriously disappearing from the earth at closing time. No, they have personal lives outside the doors of our offices, and it's important to know a little about those lives.

Some of my favorite moments as a boss have been based on personal moments I've shared with my employees. If they have families, I'm interested in what their kids are up to. If they've got a significant other, I like to know a little about whom they're involved with. I like to understand what kind of people they are and what they have to deal with outside of working hours.

I even help out when I can. For example, one person who was very important to my operation wanted to put his daughter in a certain preschool, but the fee was out of his reach. I offered to take care of it for him. Another person had a wife with a chronic condition that the physical therapist in town couldn't address. I found a specialist who could and told him I'd cover the expense.

Does this make me the nicest, most altruistic guy in the world? Well, I'd love to say that's the case, but in both situations I just mentioned, the employee involved was very stressed out. When someone is feeling that kind of tension, they can't do their best work. I knew that if I helped them solve those difficulties, those employees were not only going to return to their former levels of performance, but they were probably going to surpass them. That's a win for all of us.

Again, as I've stressed throughout this chapter, when you approach leadership from a positive standpoint rather than a negative one, you create loyalty and you motivate effort. When you reward your people for reaching goals, you can really inspire them to a new level of accomplishment.

Last year I did something I called a "100-Day Sprint," which was a concentrated effort to reach some short-term goals. I told the guy running it for me that if we all reached our targets in that one hundred days, I would send him and his family on a vacation anywhere he wanted within the continental United States. Well, we hit the bullseye, so off they went to San Diego and Anaheim for a great couple of weeks. It was much better than offering him a bonus or raise because I made it about what he and his family wanted, not some arbitrary thing I decided for them.

The rules above reflect my overall philosophy of leadership, and that philosophy revolves around interacting with your people in a positive, pro-active, and encouraging way. I don't believe in bullying employees. It creates unnecessary tension, dilutes teamwork, and makes everyone miserable. You also end up driving out your best employees, leaving you with a bunch of "yes-men" who aren't about growing themselves or your company but are only in the business of surviving the next dressing-down.

Ignoring your employees and treating them as machines instead of human beings is just as bad. When neglect is your *modus operandi*, your people end up feeling as if their efforts aren't noticed, let alone appreciated, and their morale slowly melts away.

It doesn't have to be like that. You can achieve far greater results by working with your people rather than against them. Yes, there are always challenges in these relationships, but in most cases, they can be resolved with a positive outcome for all concerned.

Leading people is a serious responsibility. I challenge you to view that responsibility as a higher calling. In the words of John Quincy Adams, the sixth President of the United States, *"If your actions inspire others to dream more, learn more, do more and become more, you are a leader."*

That's something I keep in mind every workday of my life.

# CHAPTER 6

# A CATEGORY OF ONE

One night, you want to relax and unwind, so you decide to watch a TV show. But what show? You've got hundreds of channels on your cable or satellite TV to choose from, and that's just for starters. You might also have Netflix or Amazon Video at your disposal, and those services have a huge library of original programming, movies, and vintage TV shows. Then there are all the other online content sites, like Hulu and YouTube. Depending on your set-up, you could have literally thousands of options for entertainment.

Each one of these channels is fighting like crazy for viewers' eyeballs. Each one of them must somehow stand out from the others and deliver shows that are unique to their own brand as well as appealing to enough people to get them to watch, or they'll go out of business. And if one of them does disappear from the TV landscape, most viewers will barely know the difference.

After all, there are a whole lot of other things to watch.

Here's the hard truth: An entrepreneurial business is a lot like one of those channels. Your customers or patients have a multitude of options of where to buy and who to go to, thanks in large part to the Internet. Now, more than ever, you've got to create a compelling reason to make a potential buyer choose your business over the competition.

That's why you can't get away with just "business as usual." You can't just provide the same product or service in the same way as everyone else. It's too crowded a marketplace today. It's important to be good at what you do, of course, and you'll make some sales as a result, but if you don't take the time to create a *unique and memorable* reason for people to seek you out, you're going to find you're swimming upstream against a powerful current. This brings us to my next rule...

## IDEAL BUSINESS RULE #9: STAND OUT FROM THE CROWD, OR YOU'LL GET LOST IN IT.

In the previous chapter, we talked about leadership from a personal standpoint. This chapter (and the next few after this one) will focus on how to make your company a leader in its sector. Making your business a Category of One not only creates that leader position, but, when done correctly, puts customer motivation into your business model right from the get-go.

So let's talk about how to get that done.

### *Big Innovation, Big Success*

*Disruption* is a popular word in the business community these days. Uber has completely upended the taxicab model. Likewise, Airbnb is a completely different take on the hotel and motel business. These twenty-first-century upstart start-ups took on industries that had barely changed how they did business for decades—and completely overhauled them. That kind of creative, out-of-the-box thinking resulted in massive success stories, not only for those companies but a lot of others like them.

It's a little soon for another rule, but to me, this one is huge and represents a fact every entrepreneur needs to keep in mind:

## IDEAL BUSINESS RULE #10: IT DOESN'T COST ANYTHING TO THINK!

Now, I know that seems obvious, but too many people barrel ahead with a business idea without taking time to think through and develop the kind of unique creative strategy that will enable them to shine more brightly than other similar companies. Pausing to put together that strategy could be the most important investment you'll make, because your Return on Investment (ROI) for coming up with a memorable business approach can be limitless. When you become a Category of One, you essentially are stepping away from the common categories your competitors would fall into and creating your own new category. You are innovating and creating a first-mover advantage that allows you to be viewed differently than everyone else by the marketplace. You set the pace. Others may copy you, but consumers will know you're the real deal. The value of that kind of leadership is priceless.

To me, putting yourself in a Category of One is essential to running an IDEAL Business. I found that out for myself with my very first full-time job when I was working for a small state college with not much in the way of money or resources. Those limitations ended up not mattering. What mattered was that I had to come up with the right plan to grow success—and then put it into action.

When I was twenty-three, I became the youngest college baseball coach in the nation, an unofficial title I held for a couple years. The program I was taking over was, in a word, *awful*. Yet, five years later, we took that school's team to the top tournament in our division, the NAIA (National Association of Intercollegiate Athletes) World Series. The other teams that made it that far were considerably more well-funded than we were. They each had about twelve scholarship players—we had less than two. But, there we were at the World Series as one of the best teams in the division.

How did we go so far with so little? We made ourselves a Category of One.

### A New Marketing Mandate

As I said, when the school named me coach, I didn't inherit much of a program. To turn things around, I needed to recruit some awesome high school talent. To put it in business terms, those star players were the "customers" I had to convince to "buy" from me. At the time, my school was far from being a Category of One. It was more like a Category of None. On paper there wasn't one good reason a top athlete would seriously consider us.

The other schools had much bigger budgets than I did. We didn't even have our own field; we used a city-owned park. Heck, I wasn't breaking even on this deal. In my first year as a college coach I was paid a grand total of three thousand dollars. I had to piecemeal other income together by doing all sorts of odd jobs. I announced volleyball games, I gave private lessons, and I served as the strength and conditioning coach for the school athletes.

The question I had to answer was *how could I bring a high caliber of talent to my team?* What would make them *want* to come to us? Clearly, I had to do something with the program that other schools weren't doing. The good news was that wouldn't be too difficult. Most baseball coaches in our division were doing pretty much the same thing, so if I did *anything* markedly different, we'd stand out like a sore thumb. The bad news was there was no money to invest in the kind of transformation we needed.

But, as I said, thinking doesn't cost a thing. I realized, neither did changing up how we marketed ourselves to our prospects. I could reinvent our brand, what our program was known for, and doing so wouldn't cost a penny.

My inner marketer awakened within me for the first time. Star athletes were our "customers," I had to figure out what would make them "buy" from us, so I asked myself, "What does a kid want out of baseball at the college level?" There was an obvious answer: Those kids want to win games, and they want to look good while doing it so they have a shot at playing professionally. Well, you couldn't help but look good if you were hitting .400 and maybe knocking out fifteen home runs in a season—maybe even going on to become an All-American. That's how you could impress scouts and maybe go on to a real career in the game.

Making that happen was right in my wheelhouse because I knew what kind of training it would take to make my kids stronger hitters. Because of my double duty as the strength and conditioning coach, I knew this was an area where baseball lagged at the time. If I brought into our program the advantages I knew strength training would deliver, our hitters could end up dominating the division. I had nothing to lose, so I decided that would be our mandate—and we would aggressively pursue it.

## The IDEAL Prospect

In the next chapter, we're going to talk in detail about the concept of discovering who your most likely customers or patients are and then building your IDEAL Business around that kind of person's wants and needs. In our case, we were after kids who wanted to do some big league hitting, so emphasizing power hitting in our program was exactly the right way to recruit the kinds of kids who were most likely to join our team.

Here's how we came to that conclusion: Our state-funded school was located in an economically depressed area that had a lot of first-generation college students. We weren't going to get kids from affluent areas or rich parents; these were guys from blue-collar or lower-middle-class backgrounds. Most of them kind of had chips on their shoulders because they had been overlooked by bigger, more well-known schools. They wanted a chance to show their stuff in the most powerful way possible.

I knew that these players would be just the kinds of guys who would be attracted to our message of strength conditioning as a primary tool of player development. They wouldn't get all that excited about the nuances of what's called "small ball," which involved scoring runs through deliberate and methodical tactics like bunting and hit-and-run. No, they wanted to score with one swing of the bat—by smashing home runs and clearing the bases in the process.

We encouraged that kind of aggressive mentality. And we worked to create the kind of environment where we could play to these kids' strengths so they'd be excited about playing for us, making them easier to recruit. It turned out to be the philosophy I still use for my businesses today: Play to your strengths, create a marketing plan that's attractive to people you want to recruit, and go get it in front of them.

**The Marketing Edge**

Because our player development program was now so different from the rest, I was no longer directly competing with other schools I couldn't outspend. Now I just had to run a baseball camp and feature this new mandate in the camp's brochure with copy that said something like, "Hey, come learn the hitting system that helped this player go from getting two hits as a high school senior to nineteen hits as a junior in college." I sent out brochures to all the potential prospects I had my eye on. That meant I didn't have to spend money on recruiting. I would instead get these kids to come to me and actually pay for the privilege by participating in my baseball camp.

When it came to recruiting, we handled that differently than other schools too; I wanted us to focus on our strengths. While other college's sports programs were using the same type of generic recruiting letter, mine was more like a sales letter. I targeted those kids with whom I actually had a shot. No way was I going to have a chance with, say, a 6'3" pitcher that threw ninety-two mph, not with one-sixth the scholarship money as everyone else. No, I would go after a 5'10" pitcher who hadn't gotten any other offers, but was determined to show the other schools they had been wrong about him. I wanted the player who was hungry and whose drive we could use to enhance his talents and skills with our strength improvement program. That was the kind of player I knew we could help achieve dramatic improvement as an athlete.

So we wouldn't have the league's greatest pitcher. It didn't matter. The other teams only had one real ace on their squads, so yeah, they would probably dominate us in that one game. But I knew if we made it into a conference tournament, there were four or five games they would have to win over us to advance. We could win enough of those games with our hitting to keep moving up. We might win those games 12-7 instead of 3-1, but a "W" is a "W," no matter what the score ends up being.

That was our plan, and it worked better than we could have imagined. It turned out to be this wonderful merging of forces where we found the right guys who bought into our mandate and ended up delivering big time. They almost always got to swing big without ever having to worry about executing the perfect bunt. As a matter of fact, in the whole season during the year we ended up going to that NAIA World Series, our team only bunted twice—and one of those times was because the player misread a signal.

Our record that year was forty-eight wins and sixteen losses.

### *Lessons Learned*

So, yes, I talked a lot of baseball in this chapter, but I did so because everything I relayed applies to business and how to put yours in a Category of One. This was a real-world scenario where I didn't have money or resources, but it didn't matter. We had the right plan, and that's what lead to our success.

I didn't know it at the time, but I approached my time as a baseball coach the same as an entrepreneur should approach a business. That's because I needed to market the school's program—just as business owners must market what they're offering—in order to succeed. When you spend seven years as a college baseball coach, your livelihood is based on being able to recruit players that will help you win. That's a tall order when you have to ask parents to send their son to your program and all you have to offer is $500 in scholarship money. You're basically asking *them* to invest tens of thousands of dollars in their child's next four years so he can play in your program, and that's a tough sell. We made it work as well as we did because we offered something the other folks couldn't. We made it work because we provided a huge benefit to those kids, a strength conditioning regimen and a chance to show their stuff, two big things that they weren't going to get anywhere else.

Whatever business you're in (or want to get into), you must find a way to deliver advantages that stand out to your prospects and that make you a true Category of One. Making this happen isn't about throwing around a lot of money on advertising. The most important element is creating a business and a marketing strategy with a singular purpose, one that pulls in the potential customer and makes them say, "Wow, these guys can really deliver on this! I've got to try it out."

Now, you're probably wondering how you can do all that for your business. Well, in the next couple of chapters, you're going to find out. In the next chapter, I'll show you how to zero in on your potential customers or patients and meet their wants and needs. In Chapter 8, I'll show you how to then transform your Category-of-One decisions into a brand message that's irresistible to your audience.

And I'm going to do that because I'm *still* all about helping people hit home runs!

## CHAPTER 7

# YOUR IDEAL NICHE

As a baseball coach, I created a program *specifically designed* to grab the attention of the kids I knew I wanted to recruit, kids who didn't want to waste time on the nuances of the sport, but instead wanted to slam the ball as hard as they could. That way they had the best shot at becoming high-visibility players. By meeting their desires, I was able to bring some strong talent onto our team and build a foundation for success.

This chapter is about helping you do the same for your business. When you're determining how to put your business in a Category of One, it's important to prioritize the wants and needs of your desired customers or patients over and above your own personal wish list. If you're not working toward their interests—if you're only interested in doing what you want to do with your company—then people are going to be much less inclined to seek you out.

Your goal, is to figure out who you want to sell to (if applicable) and what's going to draw them to your business. The typical conversations about customers, however, can get very confusing. Entrepreneurs throw around words like "IDEAL Client," "Target Market" and "Niche" and use them interchangeably as if they mean the same thing. It's an easy mistake to make, and I've been guilty of it myself. But when you precisely define those terms and use them the way they were meant to be used, you put yourself on a course to accurately pinpoint who your best potential customers or patients are—and how to appeal to them.

So, before we go much further, let's look at the definition of those buzz words. I want you to understand what each one really means and what impact they can make on your business. As I do that, you'll also see how these distinct facets create a three-stage formula for successfully transforming your business into a customer magnet.

### Your IDEAL Client

The first stage of that formula begins with nailing down who your IDEAL Client is.

Your IDEAL Clients are the customers or patients who are real superstars to your business, the people who are really into what you do and how you do it. They're incredibly enthusiastic about you and appreciative of the products and services you offer. They're not shy about singing your praises to others they know. They see you as more than a business. To them, you are a positive force in their lives because of what you provide for them.

Although IDEAL Clients probably only comprise, at most, about 10 percent of your client base at any given time, as frequent "buyers", they contribute a much bigger percentage than that to your bottom line. They're the kind of people you can't help but wish you had a lot more of. They represent those who are going to have the most passion for buying from you, which is why your first step in this process should be getting to know who they are.

Now, when I say you want to get to know who they are, I'm not talking about their demographics, such as where they live or how much money they make. That's going to come later. For the moment, this is about discovering their intangibles, such as what kinds of personalities and traits they might have in common. From there you can begin to construct your "typical" IDEAL Client, the kind of person to whom you should reach out with your marketing because you'll have an excellent chance of making a connection with them.

Of course, it may be hard for you to determine these intangibles if you're not providing a personal service where you encounter clients or patients one on one. In that case, you may want to survey customers with some general questions to find out if they share common interests, hobbies, charitable endeavors, goals, or other attributes related to your specific business.

Because IDEAL Clients are a driving (and profitable) force behind your business, it just makes sense to find out as much as you can about them—so you can bring in a lot more like them. Also, if you zoom in on what they like best about you—and what other kinds of services or products they might also enjoy, you can uncover a lot of valuable insight into your business in the process. The results of studying these people often gives you a valuable map for moving your business forward.

### Your Target Market

Once you've identified your typical IDEAL Client, your next step is to define your Target Market.

Your Target Market is based on a set of demographics that represent the most attractive pool of prospects for your business. These are the people to whom you want to market. For example, you might be after Dads aged twenty-eight to forty who live in a three-mile radius and have a household income of $100,000 or more. Or retirees with lots of disposable income who regularly purchase luxury products. You can put together countless demographic combinations depending on what you're providing and who's most likely to buy it. Big data can provide you with an overwhelming amount of information these days. But, as a small businessperson, your best bet is to keep your Target Market as simple as possible.

Your IDEAL Client type will give you the best clues as to how to narrow down the data to create a manageable Target Market— just be sure to focus on what demographics they share. You'll be able to quickly see what categories jump out at you. For example, they may live in similar neighborhoods, fall in the same age group, have similar incomes, and be mostly of one gender.

Or not! You may find that the only demographic data your IDEAL Clients have in common is generational—they're all Millennials, Gen X-ers, Baby Boomers, or some combination of those broad generational categories. Or it might come down to a much more specific type like my wife's first business, Fit Yummy Mummy, which targets busy young moms who want to get in shape after giving birth.

Whatever the case, you want to get specific with your Target Market because unless you're Coca-Cola or McDonalds, it's a waste of money to try and sell yourself to the entire world. (By the way, even those corporate behemoths create different messaging for different Target Markets.) There are always going to be people who will never come to you simply because they have no interest in what you're providing. You don't try to sell cars to people who don't drive, nor do you try to sell steaks to vegetarians—so why throw away money on the attempt? The best way to market the most affordably and effectively is by going after the Target Market that has the most interest in what you do.

## IDEAL BUSINESS RULE #11: AIM FOR A SPECIFIC TARGET, AND YOU EMPOWER YOUR MARKETING TO HIT THE BULLSEYE.

Once you've identified your specific Target Market, the next step is to think about *what that Target Market wants*. Let's go beyond even that and try to figure out what their greatest want might be in terms of what your business does. The answer is where your sweet spot lies. If you can dial in their big *want* and make it an integral part of how you do business, you'll become a Category of One.

That's the third part of the formula for making your business a customer magnet, and it's what we're going to tackle next.

### *Your IDEAL Niche*

Traditionally, a niche is a focused group comprising the people *your business is designed to serve*—a combination of who you've determined is your IDEAL Client and your Target Market. I like to take the concept of a niche a step further and focus on finding your IDEAL *Niche*. What I mean by an IDEAL Niche is *how you best serve that combination of* IDEAL *Client and Target Market.* An IDEAL Business always aims to find that IDEAL Niche.

Let's apply the IDEAL Niche to a restaurant business, a high-end eatery whose IDEAL Client eats out once a week because (a) they don't feel like cooking for themselves every single night, and (b) they like to enjoy a quality restaurant experience.

So what do we know about these kinds of potential diners? We know that experience is very important to them, so they obviously want the restaurant to offer a great atmosphere and great food. They also want the staff to take care of them, not ignore them— these are customers who work hard and want to be rewarded with a higher level of service. Let's add one more qualifier. Let's say we determined they like the restaurant to be close to their neighborhood so they don't have to drive a long way to get there.

Those are the IDEAL Clients' characteristics. Now what about the Target Market?

Since these IDEAL customers like to eat locally, the Target Market is going to be households within maybe a five-to-ten-mile radius of the restaurant. We should probably narrow down the households to those who earn in excess of $100,000 a year. Because most people under a certain age don't earn that kind of money, we're going to go a step further and say this Target Market is made up of people ages thirty-five and up.

Our niche, then, is people who dine out regularly, who are relatively affluent, middle-aged and older, and live nearby. Those are our most likely customers and our potential IDEAL Clients, the kind of people we want to attract because they'll come in a few times a month and spend a lot when they do.

But what's our IDEAL *Niche*? How do we up the ante and make sure our restaurant is unique in a way that's going to be irresistible to those kinds of people?

There are many ways to make this happen. We can serve the kind of food that's especially appealing to this niche as well as make sure to design the kind of atmosphere they enjoy. We can also make sure the staff is friendly, welcoming, and good at bonding with diners so they'll look forward to returning and seeing them again. In all these areas, we need to make sure we surpass what similar restaurants in the area are offering.

Then, for good measure, we can look for certain special "extras" that will seal the deal with our niche. It could be a silly gimmick like singing waiters or something more substantial, like offering an outstanding wine list. Or it could mean hiring an amazing chef whose food is irresistible. It all depends on what really resonates with the restaurant's typical IDEAL Client and Target Market. Most importantly, it all depends on what our niche's greatest want is.

A little earlier, I mentioned my wife's business. It became successful because she targeted young moms and tapped into what their greatest want was, which was getting their pre-baby bodies back. But the big intangible that they were *really* after was feeling like the best versions of themselves again without a huge time commitment. These are women who've given up a little on what they look like simply because they've been too busy taking care of their kids (and maybe working a job at the same time). They want to feel and look like their pre-baby selves even though they're now much too busy to commit much time to that kind of self-improvement.

My wife's answer? She created a program that offers powerful results, and the moms only need to dedicate fifteen minutes of their day to see those results. That feels manageable to these moms, which is one of the real keys to the program's success. They stick with the program because they get their big want: a fit body in a relatively small amount of time. Making sure that your customers or patients get their big want is what puts your business into that Category of One.

When you define your IDEAL Client, your Target Market, and finally, your IDEAL Niche, you put yourself through a three-part process that sets you up to successfully reinvent yourself as a Category of One. Pause here for a moment and think about your business:

1. What are the qualities that your favorite clients or patients possess?
2. What Target Market do most of them fall into?
3. What is your Niche is when it comes to what you help them achieve and how you actually accomplish it?

This is your formula for finding and connecting with the prospects you want to serve. Now, follow through on that reinvention! Go out there and let your Target Market know about your business through aggressive marketing and branding that puts your message front and center. That's what our next chapter is all about: crafting the right brand message that will tap directly into your Category of One status. So read on, and I'll help you pull in all the IDEAL Clients you can handle.

# CHAPTER 8

# YOUR IDEAL BRAND

Once you've defined your IDEAL Niche, that group of consumers you want to attract to your business, it's time to let that IDEAL Niche know about you using your brand and the message it conveys. Now, I'm not going to tell you how to create the perfect logo or what font you should use. Sure, that stuff matters, but we're talking about the most important step in your marketing process. Before you get into any of that marketing minutia, you want to figure out how to attract the people you want as clients, customers or patients. This is done by promoting the unique advantages you've established in your Category of One.

As you can see, you will be building on the work you've already done as outlined in this book thus far. If you've made yourself a Category of One in ways that matter to consumers, they will respond to marketing messages that specifically zero in on those services, products, or experiences that meet their needs. In the process of delivering a unique and authentic message, you're also going to attract many more of the kinds of customers or patients who fit your IDEAL Client category.

In many ways, marketing is about controlling how your business is perceived by the public. Your branding should be telling potential (and existing) customers and patients, "Look, this is who we are, and this is how we're different." It shouldn't be about constantly trumpeting discounts or copying the advertising of the guy down the street. Which brings us to the next rule:

## IDEAL BUSINESS RULE #12: MAKE YOUR MARKETING AS SINGULAR AS YOUR BUSINESS.

Here's why I think this rule is so important: When you've gone to the trouble to make your business different in an authentic and meaningful way, it just doesn't make sense to not extend that same effort to your branding. It would be like if Uber made all their drivers paint their cars to look like yellow cabs. The whole company's point is to *not* be an old-school taxi service. You *want* to show everyone how you're different. That's what's going to bring them to your door.

That's why you want to avoid one-size-fits-all marketing. During my days in the fitness industry, I would see the exact same ad copy used by different trainers and boot camps. By using the exact same message, they weren't giving prospective clients or patients any reason to choose one or the other. They all seemed interchangeable—and that's the exact opposite of what you want for your branding.

You have no way of building any type of long-term following or loyalty if you present yourself the same as everybody else. If somebody else comes along and they simply undercut your price by a few bucks, you've given people no reason to work with you. When you present yourself in a generic way, people don't mind buying from you—but they also don't mind buying from someone else!

### *Uncovering Your Branding Basics*

Here are three main points your branding and marketing should tackle head on:

- Attracting your IDEAL Niche
- Expressing your unique advantages
- Letting the market know what you and your business stand for

Let's take those one at a time.

To begin with, your brand must be customized so that it attracts that IDEAL Niche we discussed in the last chapter. That's first and foremost. It doesn't matter if you love what your company does and how it does it. If your branding doesn't attract the clients or patients you want and who are most likely to buy from you, then you've got to retool it. If you can't attract the right prospects for your business, you're in trouble before you even start.

Secondly, your branding needs to express your unique advantages. What do you have to offer that your competition doesn't? That's what's going to set you apart as a Category of One, so naturally your marketing needs to sell that essential aspect of your business. Your market message could be based on your delivery system, on your track record, on your specific products or services, or a combination of all those, and your brand should be designed to attract the kind of people that would gravitate to those advantages.

Finally, your brand needs to let the market know what you and your business stand for. You don't want to be weak with your message or try to be all things to all people. Instead, you want people to know what they can expect when they come to do business with you, and whom you're designed to serve (and just as importantly, whom you *aren't* designed to serve). That second part is just as important as the first part. If you can't be clear about to whom your business is catering, you're not specialized enough. I'll talk more about specialization a little later in this chapter and why it's essential for an entrepreneur.

For now, let's go through a couple of important exercises that will help you zero in on these points.

The first exercise is short and simple. Start by answering the following three questions:

- What are you known for?
- What makes you memorable? Unique?
- What do you get compliments on?

Answering these questions helps you further articulate your platform and gets you clear about who you are and what you're doing. Now that I've got you thinking about those points, let's further refine your brand into a single thought. Simply fill in the blanks of these statements:

I help _____.

What do I help them do? _____.

For example, if I were to complete this exercise, I would end up with this basic business statement: I help entrepreneurs build their IDEAL Business.

This is the statement I use when someone asks me what I do. I could just say, "Oh, well, I'm a business consultant," and the person making the inquiry might just nod and move on. However, when I answer, "I help entrepreneurs build their IDEAL Business," it inspires a bunch of other questions, such as "What is an IDEAL Business?" "How do you help entrepreneurs do this?" and so forth.

This statement also sets me up as a person who creates *a definable benefit for others*, and that's obviously very attractive to someone who is in the category of client I serve. An entrepreneur would instantly wonder how I might improve their business with my system, and that in turn would motivate a conversation, a conversation that could end up being very valuable to both of us.

The point here is that you need to define yourself beyond just your job title or occupation. A job title is boring, it's bland, it's generic, and these are all things you want to avoid in representing yourself to others. The "I help" type of statement creates an instant marketing message that immediately hooks those who might need your services.

## Your Perfect Five-Point Formula for Marketing

The second exercise I'd like you to do will enable you to expand on that basic branding statement you just completed. By answering the following five questions, you will have a perfect "Five-Point Formula" that will provide the complete foundation for all of your marketing messaging moving forward.

1. Whom do you want to help?
2. What is their pain? What do they want?
3. How do you deliver the solution?
4. What are the results of the solution you provide?
5. Why should they choose you?

If you can answer all five of the above questions in an effective manner, you will have the messaging you need for all your marketing: everything from brochures to direct mail campaigns to Internet banner ads. It's very important to be able to answer all five. When you can't, you're allowing for some very significant holes in your marketing process.

Here's an example: Let's say your company creates websites for businesses. And you're very clear about the answer to Question 1, whom you want to help (small local businesses), as well as Question 3, how you provide the solution (you think they need sophisticated and attractive website designs). But you went ahead and skipped right over Question 2, what your IDEAL Niche really wants. In this case, let's say that niche really wants websites that effectively convert prospects to customers or patients.

As you can see, what you want is totally different from what your customers or patients want. That kills your marketing right out of the gate.

Here's why: You go on and heavily promote your ability to provide elegant and high-level website design, saying the benefit is the kind of design that makes a small business look more high-level. But the local businesses you're trying to reach completely misread your message. To them, high-level design means (a) you're probably too expensive, and (b) you're not properly focused on the sales results they need. The result is that your marketing actually causes businesses to *turn away* from you.

Many entrepreneurs make the crucial mistake of emphasizing what *they* think is important for their clients or patients instead of what the clients or patients think is important. They want a solution to alleviate their pain points; they don't care as much about the mechanism that gets them there. In our example, you may be right about those local businesses needing a more upscale look, but if they don't agree, it doesn't matter. So you need to reframe your solution to their problem in a way that reflects *their* concerns.

Similarly, if you don't address Question 4, the results of your solution, you may be ignoring another powerful marketing point. In the last chapter I told you about my wife's successful business helping busy moms get back into shape. One of her typical prospects might claim that all she wants to do is lose fifteen pounds, but as I noted, the real results she's after might be to feel better about herself, regain the confidence she had before she had the baby, and to have a better relationship with her spouse.

If that's the case, then you can emphasize those "ultimate benefits" in your marketing and trigger a stronger response from your IDEAL Niche. You can use testimonials that validate those benefits and provide social proof. In contrast, if you just focus on losing weight, some prospects won't see those ultimate benefits. They'll only think about having to exercise... and they'll turn away from your services. It's a lot easier to turn on Netflix than to do even a short workout, but if you show your niche how that workout will significantly improve their lives, that's a strong motivator to avoid a binge-watch and start exercising.

Question 5, of course, goes back to our Category of One objective: Why should your IDEAL Niche choose you? What motivates them to seek you out and stay with you? All too often a business defaults to price or location as its reason for being. "We're cheap and we're close." Those are the two answers you want to avoid for Question 5 because anyone can beat you at that game, and it says nothing about why you're *really* special.

For your answer to Question 5, it's much better to focus on how you're a specialist. If you look at the field of medicine, we all know that a specialist gets paid a lot more than a general practitioner. That rule applies to other industries as well. *That's because people will pay more for solutions that are specific to them.* They feel their individual needs are being addressed by a person who has experience with them, and that increases the value of your product or service in their minds. The way that I think about this and explain it is that I would much rather be the king of a very small island than somebody who's anonymous in a land of millions.

Many entrepreneurs fear being too specific about what they do. They should instead worry about being too broad with their intended niche. I understand this can be a hard pill to swallow as an entrepreneur. Naturally, you want to help everyone as best as you can (and of course, make as many sales as possible in the process). But dominating a small vertical market gives you the credibility and confidence to grow. Besides, once you own a small slice of a market, you can always expand by degrees and scoop up more and more slices for yourself because you've already proven yourself.

I want to emphasize how important it is for you to come up

with the best possible answers to those five questions on page 111 because they are the foundation of everything you do from a marketing standpoint. If you dig deep for the right answers, you're bound to strike oil.

Here's just one way your five-point formula answers will serve you: We all want our business to generate referrals. We all want the kind of word-of-mouth that brings in new customers, patients and clients on a regular basis. But if we can't articulate what makes our businesses stand out, if we can't quickly and simply relate what we do and how we're different, how can we expect others to do it? How is our team, our customers, our patients, our network of friends and family supposed to sell us effectively if we can't do it? This is such an important idea that…well, it deserves its own rule.

## IDEAL BUSINESS RULE #13:
## IF YOU CAN'T EXPLAIN WHY YOUR BUSINESS IS SPECIAL, NO ONE WILL KNOW IT IS!

You don't want people to just say, "Yeah, these guys are good," or give you some other bland, unmemorable endorsement and leave it at that. You want to create *champions* for your business, people who will really help move the ball forward for you. Because that's how real success happens.

Answering these five questions gives you the talking points you need to differentiate yourself and get people excited about you. That's when they end up talking about how great you are at lunch, at work, at a party, wherever and whenever—because you've enabled them to talk about you in way that's meaningful and attractive to your IDEAL Niche.

### *Make Your Brand Magnetic*

Speaking of attractive, let's talk about making your brand magnetic. We've just examined how to lay the groundwork for your IDEAL Brand. Of course, it's a critically important step. But it's still only groundwork. You still have one more important step to take, and that's making your brand *magnetic*. You do that by treating it as an active, living thing that you and your team attend to on a daily basis so that it consistently attracts the kind of people you want to draw to your business.

Remember the phrase "active, living thing" because thinking of your brand in that way should be a priority. You can't just say, "Well, we've thought out our brand, now let's move on." Instead, you must create the kind of strong and irresistible identity that creates buzz and solidifies your brand in the public's mind. Otherwise, you're going to end up like the tree that falls in the forest when nobody's around. Yeah, it's going to make a big sound, but nobody's going to hear it.

The fact is that your brand message is no good if it's only a message. If you don't make that brand a *reality* in the way you run your business, that message not only doesn't help you, it can hurt you—because you're not living up to what your brand promises.

That's why you want to establish your brand standards before you start marketing your brand. Yes, you can say you want to be known for certain things, but is the actual experience that clients or patients have with you reflective of those things? Is what you do consistent with what you're saying? If you're promising certain results with your product or service, are people actually enjoying those results? If you want to say your service is the best in your industry, have you taken the steps to make sure that's the truth?

This is the last link of a chain we started when we talked about your business being an extension of who you are and what you want out of life. Ideally, as an entrepreneur, your values must be reflected in your company. Otherwise, your business or business model is not a great fit for you. Now it's time to take that idea a step further and make sure you deliver the values you've defined for your brand in a consistent and congruent manner to your customers and patients.

Here's an exercise that will help with that effort. Ask yourself these questions:

### What do you want to be known for?

You'll find the answers to this question in your IDEAL Brand brainstorming you did last chapter. Review your business operation and see how well you're living up to the perception you want to convey.

### Why did your best clients, patients, or customers choose you?

Don't ignore what your superstar clients or patients already love about you. Keep on doing the things that drive the most enthusiasm from them.

### What is the #1 thing you want to be known for to your IDEAL Niche?

Hopefully, you already know this from the Five-Point Formula for Marketing questions. Just remember, your #1 thing must be something that both you and your customers or patients are pumped about and that you can position front-and-center in your business.

### What do you have to change to be known for your #1 thing?

The changes you make to reflect that #1 thing will likely entail a combination of marketing and operational adjustments. As an entrepreneur, you have the power to make those adjustments—and they need to be made across the board.

Your brand message isn't just represented by a slogan or brochure. It also must be an integral part of the services you provide, the products you sell, and the overall experience you're creating through the people who represent your business in one way or another. For example, a popular brand message for a small business these days, in this time of huge, detached corporate transactions, is that you're big on one-on-one relationships and delivering great customer service.

If that's your brand message, you need to make sure that when somebody walks in your front door, you greet them with a smile and engage in a conversation that creates a connection. Even better, make your customers or patients feel like family. If the phone rings, make sure it gets answered by the second ring and, if for some reason nobody can get to the phone, you have a policy of calling everyone back within a certain (short) time frame.

These things may seem trivial, but they're not to the people you serve. You can't say you've got a relationship-oriented business but act like you're mainly transactional. It's easy to throw out buzzwords like "dependable," "friendly," and "reliable." But when a customer leaves a message and nobody gets back to them in three days, those words ring hollow to the people who matter the most: the ones who buy from you.

## IDEAL BUSINESS RULE #14: IF YOU CAN'T LIVE UP TO YOUR BRAND, YOU DON'T REALLY HAVE ONE.

Here's the bottom line: Whatever you say about your business, you must be able and willing to bring that talk to life. If you don't, the discrepancies will catch up with you. You can't create expectations and then not meet them, because there's nothing that's going to kill a business faster than marketing that misleads the consumer. That consumer will not give you a second chance and, more importantly, they may tell everyone they know about how you disappointed them.

Instead, create a great experience for whoever comes in contact with any aspect of your business. Believe it or not, your customer service can be a more important asset than anything you sell. Zappos, the online shoe retailer, sold the same kind of footwear as everybody else. But they made a commitment to service that, for the time, seemed truly radical and a recipe for bankruptcy. The result? It made them a billion-dollar sensation that was so successful Amazon finally bought them out.

That's the way a magnetic brand operates.

# CHAPTER 9

# YOUR IDEAL PLATFORM

So far, in terms of building your IDEAL business, we've talked about a lot of behind-the-scenes stuff: creating your brand, defining your niche, and fine tuning your basic marketing message. All of that is like getting a play ready to present to the public. Everybody's learning their lines, scenery is getting built, parts are being cast, and both the crew and the actors are rehearsing like crazy to make sure everything goes off without a hitch on opening night. Here's the problem—all that effort and preparation is for nothing if the producers haven't found a way to get an audience into the theatre to actually watch the play!

In respect to entrepreneurs, that means that even if you've created the most magnificent brand with the most amazing marketing message in the world, it won't matter unless you build a platform to communicate that brand and message to your intended IDEAL Niche.

That's why, in this chapter, we're going to talk about how to create that platform: a focused marketing system that will enable you to consistently reach out to your niche in a way that converts prospects to customers, patients and clients and, in turn, builds your business on an ongoing basis.

### The First Impression Is Not Enough

These days, your platform will almost certainly be a virtual one. In the past few decades, the Internet has revolutionized marketing, enabling anyone to instantly reach millions, even billions of people at once. Never before in the history of the world has communication on this level been a possibility for the average person.

That's the good news. The bad news is, everybody else is doing what you're trying to do, creating the ultimate Tower of Babel. There's so much online chatter out there that it's really, really easy for your message to get lost in the noise. The answer? Same as it's been throughout this book: Once again you must differentiate and ask yourself, *"How do I stand out from the competition with my communication? How can I present myself in such a way that people will pay attention to what I'm doing?"*

Fortunately, you've already done some of the heavy-lifting in this effort if you've been doing the work and answering the questions in the past few chapters. By putting your Category-of-One brand positioning to work, you'll begin to attract a steady stream of prospects to your platform. But that initial attraction won't be enough.

The real trick is to keep them interested in what you're doing— and that can be the hardest part. A platform takes time to build and even longer to really pay off; it's very much a long-term investment. Unless you're selling a miracle once-in-a-lifetime product or service, people are not going to instantly click on a "Buy Now" button when they first encounter your marketing messages.

## IDEAL BUSINESS RULE #15: WE DON'T GET TO DECIDE WHEN SOMEBODY IS READY TO BUY.

No matter how great your branding and marketing messages are, you're going to be on your prospect's schedule; they're not going to be on yours. You can't order someone to seek you out at any given moment. It can take a while to acquire new customers or patients. These statistics from the National Sales Association provide some eye-opening evidence of that fact:

- 2 percent of sales are made on the first contact
- 3 percent of sales are made on the second contact
- 5 percent of sales are made on the third contact
- 10 percent of sales are made on the fourth contact
- 80 percent of sales are made on the fifth to twelfth contact

No, we can't control when someone buys from us; however, what we can control is how people perceive us. We do that by constructing the right kind of platform—a platform that contains the right ingredients that will eventually persuade prospects to convert to customers or patients.

For more than ten years, that's just what my platform has done for me, and it has become the lifeblood of my business. I'll go into a little more detail about how it works later (it's actually a lot simpler than you might think), but first, let's tackle some basics of what your platform must accomplish and how it can accomplish them.

### The Four Pillars of a Platform

To me, there are four "pillars" that support and strengthen an entrepreneurial platform. Let's talk about them one at a time.

### Pillar #1: Attention

This pillar is really Marketing 101. Whenever we run an ad, do a public speaking gig, or promote ourselves in any way, the objective is to get people's attention. If we can't make this first step work for us, if we can't find a way to initially attract anyone to our messaging, everything stops in its tracks. Your platform needs to contain the kind of positioning and value that draws people to it. You must be able to generate that first burst of interest to begin developing a relationship.

## Pillar #2: Authority

Next, you have to successfully position yourself as one of the superstars in your field. There are a variety of ways to do that. You can do education-based marketing or provide social proof through testimonials and third-party validations. All of these tactics contain proof of your knowledge and experience. When you're seen as an authority in your field, people *want* to know what you have to say. That kind of authority automatically attracts folks to your platform and gives a big assist in helping your prospects convert to customers or patients.

## Pillar #3: Trust

Establishing authority creates the beginnings of genuine trust in you and your business. From there, as long as you're consistent, a straight-shooter, and you keep delivering value in one form or another, that trust will only continue build. The result? You become the one (and hopefully *only* one) from whom your niche wants to go to, even if your prices might be a little higher than your competition. Their trust in you gives you more value in their eyes.

## Pillar #4: Engagement

This final pillar is where a lot of entrepreneurs skip or stop building, which is dangerous because it's such a critical component of a platform. For example, let's say you start a blog site. You write three or four posts, but then you stop because you think they're not getting enough views. Or you send out a couple newsletters, decide it's not really delivering enough results and quit. It happens all too often. More and more, our society expects instant gratification. People bail out on a situation when it doesn't immediately work.

Starting a platform can seem like a very lonely business. You feel like the Maytag repairman in the old commercials, the guy who never gets a call. When you're building a platform, however, you can't expect too much too soon. It takes time to build a following. Once you have a following, you have to keep building by creating enough engagement that your followers stick around until they're ready to buy. Showing up and staying visible requires a commitment.

The Four Pillars of Platform are designed to work together to create relationships between our respective niches and us. We've got to first be able to get that niche's attention. We then must establish the kind of trust and authority that will keep its attention. Finally, we must engage with the people within our niche to such an extent that, when they are motivated to take out their credit cards or schedule an appointment, we're the ones they come to—because they believe we're providing the best solution for their needs. When we build up their confidence in us, they come to trust that we can give them the outcomes they want.

That's why the platform can become such a huge and foundational aspect of your brand. When your platform integrates your Category-of-One positioning and its marketing messaging, people will see you as "owning" a certain sector of your industry. But that doesn't happen unless you continually build your platform with fresh content.

## IDEAL BUSINESS RULE #16: ROME WASN'T BUILT IN A DAY—AND NEITHER IS A PLATFORM.

### *Choosing Your Hub*

Your platform begins by building your hub. When people do a Google search to find out more about you, more often than not, your hub is where they're going to look first. In most cases, that hub is your website so you've got to make sure your website reflects your brand and what it's all about.

That doesn't mean you have to run out and spend tens of

thousands of dollars on that website to make it blast lasers or shoot off fireworks to get people's attention. That'll probably just scare them into pulling the plug out of their computer. No, you just need to make sure your home page is congruent with your overall messaging and provides the right image and content.

Think of what happens when you go to a real-life, in-person business meeting. (I've heard these are rare nowadays, but apparently they do still occur!) Maybe you're going to meet an important client or prospect or are expecting a new patient. You're not going to wear a bathrobe and slippers to that meeting because you'd look unprofessional—or crazy. Instead, you choose clothes that help you look and feel like your best, most confident self. Even if your personal branding is more to the casual end, you choose clothes that reflect your style and put your best self forward.

The look and feel of your hub should follow suit. It must reinforce your marketing message in a strong, positive, and memorable way. If your hub seems haphazard and sloppy (e.g., lots of typos or copy that's not focused or thought out), then the visitors to your site are going to ask themselves some questions, such as these:

- Do I really want to buy from someone who cares so little about their presentation?
- How can I trust that what I buy from this person is actually going to deliver?

If they have to ask those questions, you've already sabotaged any chance of engagement with that person. Right off the bat, they are wary rather than trusting of you, what you do, and how you do it. That certainly undercuts your authority as well.

### Spreading Out to Social Media

Social media, of course, must also be an integral part of your platform strategy. Facebook and the like are so universal these days that it's easy to take your social media presence for granted. But putting your social media on auto pilot or neglecting it all together can be a huge mistake because these different platforms are excellent networking tools. Social media gives you the opportunity to connect with your audience and establish your brand with them on a day-to-day basis in a personal way that your website can't. Remember, your site is sitting out there in cyberspace all by its lonesome, and it takes someone specifically searching for it to find it. With social media, however, you're going to where the people are—billions of people who are looking for something new to connect with. You can be one of those somethings.

When you consider how to attract those in your niche, consider this: It's more than likely that everyone in your target market is on some form of social media—and most of them are on it almost 24/7. With smartphone usage soaring sky-high, people literally have their social media accounts at their fingertips at all times of the day, and many constantly check their apps on Facebook, Twitter, Instagram, Pinterest, LinkedIn, etc. If they're always on these services, you should be too.

I listed a few of the main social media sites in that previous paragraph, but there are many more specialized services out there. Frankly, a business can get lost trying to market on all of them, so try to focus on the platform that's the most relevant to what you do, and dominate it.

Here are some quick takes on the primary social media sites I mentioned:

- **Facebook** is the biggest and probably the best social media site. It is an excellent place to establish your social media base.
- **Pinterest** is great for recipes, designs, and anything primarily visual.

- The visual also dominates on **Instagram**, since it's all photo based.
- **LinkedIn** is the place to go for business-to-business marketing because you're only dealing with professionals.
- **Twitter** is primarily useful to lead people to other, more substantial social media posts. It's hard to really say much using only 140 characters.

In all likelihood, Facebook is where you want to be. That's where you can run a gift card contest, thank a great customer, announce a new product or service, profile people on your staff, and drive folks to your website. It's also a chance to build your reputation as an online expert where you can share links to your content that demonstrate your expertise and provide short "daily tips" that deliver a small pop of value to your audience.

Some people struggle to provide regular content for their social media pages. This is where you should feel free to repurpose stuff from your website, your blogsite, your marketing emails, your books, videos, or any type of content you're generating to bolster your expert status. You can also create relevant, funny or meaningful memes through countless free meme generators accessible online. If you're good at creating memes, leverage that talent! Impactful memes spread like wildfire. Pictures and videos always spur more activity, such as likes, shares, and views, compared to just straight text. Keep that in mind, too, when you're posting on your social media sites.

Finally, social media is at its best when it creates dynamic conversations. So follow up and respond to posts about your business as well as comments on your page. Try to create engagement whenever possible. Yes, the Internet can be a little like the Wild West in that you never know when somebody's going to try to gun you down, but keep your end of social media conversations as positive as possible—and duck out gracefully if things get ugly. If a dissatisfied customer pops up publicly on your page in an effort to disrupt your messaging, ask them to message you privately. Then attempt to resolve the complaint out of the public eye.

### Connecting People to Your Platform: The Lead Magnet Strategy

Once your hub is built and your social media presence is secure, you'll want to find ways to attract your niche to your platform. That's where the lead magnet strategy comes into play. You want to grab people's attention? Using a lead magnet is a good way to do it—if done correctly.

A lead magnet is something of interest or value that you provide, usually free of charge, to a potential customer of your business. Whatever you're offering must be of so much interest or value that a prospect is willing to give you their contact information in order to get it. This, in turn, allows you to make them a part of your platform and engage with them on a regular basis.

Generally, a lead magnet is some kind of educational product, such as a special report, eBook, or video that is (a) directly relevant to your business and (b) has an enticing title that promises to answer a burning question or satisfy an urgent need. Why an educational product? Because it's a great way to claim your authority and demonstrate your expertise.

Of course, most people aren't really all that excited about getting an educational product, even it's free. (You probably didn't do cartwheels when the teacher gave out free textbooks on the first day of class, either.) That's why your lead magnet must be squarely focused on one or more of your niche's wants and needs. As a veteran of the fitness business, I can tell you from experience that giving away a freebee explaining the best way to do a dead lift exercise will never be as successful as a PDF entitled "How to Get into Your Skinny Jeans in 30 Days or Less."

People are cautious about giving away their contact info these days and with good reason. Their email addresses end up on a lot of marketing lists, then their inboxes start overflowing with spam. Your lead magnet has to seem worth that risk to a prospect; they have to feel like the information you're providing is important enough to them to allow you to market to them. It doesn't have to be a five hundred-page book or even a fifty-page book. Frankly, you can make a great lead magnet out of five pages of content if it's the right five pages. Most people are too busy to handle more. You can also make a lead magnet out of a webinar, a video, or even a slide show.

### The Lead Magnet That Repels Instead of Attracts

So a lead magnet seems like a simple and effective strategy to get leads, right? It doesn't require any commitment beyond providing an email address because there's no money involved—and it's easy to promote through Facebook and other online marketing. All you need to do is trumpet your enticing title and wait for the clicks to come in.

And yet... this is where lot of entrepreneurs make a fatal mistake.

Any relationship must start out on the right foot. You don't show up for a date holding a bouquet of dead flowers, right? Well, too often a lead magnet can end up being about as appealing as a dozen rotting roses. That happens when entrepreneurs don't put enough care into what they're giving away.

It starts when their mind-set causes them to think, *I need to capture people's contact information.* It may seem a little silly, but the word "capture" really bothers me. It makes it sound too much like a hostage situation, like you're trying to take innocent people hostage with your marketing, trapping them and putting them at your mercy. It makes lead gathering seem less than a real above-board trade, an equal exchange of value. The result of that kind of attitude can result in creating a lead magnet that is, to put it bluntly, a piece of crap.

How many of you have ever downloaded a freebee online because the landing page looked really good? You saw it and said to yourself, *Man, this looks awesome!* It seemed to be promising you the world in a PDF. Then you downloaded it, and it was terrible. I mean, TERRIBLE. It looked like it was formatted, written, and designed by a kindergarten class, and it contained no information that you couldn't have figured out for yourself.

When that happens, you feel like you were tricked. And your attitude toward the marketer is, "Okay...you fooled me. You got my e-mail address. But you know what? You're not getting anything else. You're not getting my time. You're not getting my attention. You're not getting my money." Suddenly that lead magnet is actually an anchor—an anchor that sinks any hope of ever getting that person back in your good graces again.

One of my guidelines for a lead magnet has been to give away something that's worth paying for. That starts the relationship on a hugely positive note, and it can still end up as a minimal cost for you on your side.

For instance, my wife, Holly, published a cookbook that racked up over $40,000 in sales. We had tangible proof that people were willing to pay for that cookbook, so we felt great about using it as a lead magnet for her business. Those leads obviously felt pretty good about getting a real book for free. That created some real positive vibes because we delivered something more than we had to. Those leads then became a lot more open to what we had to say next because there was real value in what we gave them.

"Value" is a big part of the lead magnet equation. Yours should contain a lot of it. It makes your giveaway stand out from other offers, and it also makes you look good in consumers' eyes. Most importantly, it's a very easy, low-barrier way to begin a relationship. So position yourself as an authority by including good, hard, and compelling information in your lead magnet. Make sure they feel as though they're getting a lot from you just for typing in their email address. When you do that, your lead magnet represents the beginning of a beautiful relationship.

Speaking of relationships ... well, that's our next chapter.

# CHAPTER 10

# THE IDEAL RELATIONSHIP

Thanks to your targeted branding and a valuable and enticing lead magnet, people are showing up at your virtual door. That's fantastic. Now, how do you convince them to stay? How do you get them to understand that it's worth their time to develop a relationship with you? How do you create the kind of ongoing value that will continue to interest them until they finally decide to buy?

Building a positive and productive business relationship isn't all that different from developing relationships with our favorite friends and family members. If we treat people with respect and show an interest in who they are and what they want, they'll feel appreciated and will want to be around us. If we act like we couldn't care less about them, however, they'll drift away until they disappear for good.

It's as simple as this:

**IDEAL BUSINESS RULE #17: IF WE DON'T PROVIDE VALUE TO A LEAD, THEY WON'T BE INCLINED TO PAY US ANY MIND.**

### Knowing and Engaging Your Niche

Communicating through your platform only works if you understand who your audience is and what their interests are.

With that insight, you can appeal to their interests in a way they'll be eager to respond to. In Chapter 7, we looked at why you need to discover the attributes of your IDEAL Niche (your most likely customers or patients) and what they might want from a business like yours. Hopefully you made some notes about your customer's or patient's wants and needs, because now we're going to put that valuable information into action.

Before we look at your business specifically, consider this illustration and how businesses connect with you: Imagine that you're watching TV (the old fashioned programing that still has commercials). You see a number of different kinds of car advertisements and notice that, although the car commercials are all selling the same thing—a car—each company is marketing their particular vehicles in their own particular way. Subaru hits hard on its safety record. Ford pushes the awesome power of its trucks. Cadillac wants to sell upscale as cool. Nissan is selling an incredible driving experience, and Buick wants you to know its cars *ain't* what Buicks used to be. Each of these companies is trying to share a message that connects with what it believes is important to its prospective customers.

These car manufacturers have done tons of market research to determine every vehicle's IDEAL Niche, which is why each model has a commercial tailored specifically to that niche. You'll see very few commercials that simply proclaim, "This car is good." No, they're going after specific demographic groups and the individual needs, wants, and preferences of that group. A successful platform must take the same approach.

You must present yourself in a way that encourages connection with your audience—you must be somebody they want to hear from (and ultimately work with). And you can't be truly magnetic to the public unless you provide "the personal touch" and demonstrate to those within your IDEAL Niche that you get them.

The ability for a business owner to create personal connections with clients, prospects or patients is becoming a lost art. We rely too heavily on technology to maintain connections and neglect to really think about what the person on the other end is all about. As an entrepreneur, you understand that nobody wants to buy from someone they don't like and don't trust. But what are you doing to help them know, like and trust you? Building positive relationships with your customers or patients is crucial to your business's success. To be successful at connecting (and at maintaining customer or patient relationships), you need to do three things:

## Be Likeable

When you're *likeable*, you've taken the first step toward being *magnetic*. People will enjoy dealing with you. So avoid being negative or snippy in your content or in your social media posts. Be positive and always offer answers. When you don't know the answers, send them to someone who does because that impresses people. Have a sense of humor, and don't take yourself too seriously—but be serious about following through on your brand messaging.

## Be Visible

If you really want to make a personal connection with your audience, you must show up where your customers, patients and prospects are already hanging out. We can be the greatest at what we do; we can be likeable, and have authority, and all that other good stuff, but if our IDEAL Niche is unable to see any of that in action, it doesn't really matter, does it? That's why social media should be an integral part of your platform. Make the effort to show up where your audience is.

## Deliver Consistent Value

To develop the strongest possible long-term connections, you must *add value often* and *show up consistently*. And you must do these things in tandem. Doing one or the other doesn't do the trick. If you deliver value every few months or so, your audience may find the content interesting, but between interactions, they may well forget you exist. On the other hand, if you keep showing up with something new every day, but that something new is just a sales pitch (or something about your cat), people are going to first tune you out and then just plain turn you off. They'll be unfollowing, unsubscribing, and doing whatever it takes to get you out of their inbox if your content doesn't provide any value to their lives.

When you provide consistent value, however, people look forward to what you're going to come up with next. Even when you have an occasional post or video that's not all that great, they'll forgive you because you've already demonstrated that most of the time, you're delivering something interesting instead of just offering "empty calories."

When you get this process of delivering consistent value down, the four pillars of your platform get built pretty quickly. If you remember, those pillars are *attention, authority, trust, and engagement*. Here is how you bring them into the mix: You retain your audience's attention by regularly posting information that's related to their interests. You gain authority because every day (or every few days) you prove your expertise. You gain trust because you're delivering value consistently over time. All of these activities lead to stronger engagement and deeper connection with your platform.

The end result of all that work is you are being seen as a person who's making your audience's lives a little better day by day. That's what really motivates your audience to keep reading your posts and watching your videos; it's what also deepens their respect for who you are and what you do to grow. Eventually, your relationship gets to a point where there's no reason they *wouldn't* buy from you when they're ready.

As you build your platform and your connection with your IDEAL Niche, here are a few other important elements to consider.

## Stick to a Schedule

Set a schedule you know you can meet and stick to it. For example, I'm big on making sure my email newsletter gets sent every single day. In ten years, I've missed that newsletter schedule a grand total of zero times. That might be too much for you, but you should show up as often as possible and on a dependable schedule. Whether it's a certain number of Facebook posts each week, how often you blog, or how frequently you post a new video, be consistent so the people who follow you know when to expect to hear from you.

By the way, following through on this kind of schedule not only adds value to your audience, it adds value to you. The more you generate content, the more you show up consistently, the better you will get at communicating and marketing yourself. I can say that with confidence because that's definitely how it's worked for me. Sticking to a schedule trains you to generate quality content on a regular basis. You'll know when you should start cranking up to deliver your brilliance to your niche, and you'll suddenly have developed a very productive and positive habit.

## Play to Your Strengths

I talked a bit about the importance of playing to your strengths already, and in this arena of connecting, it's something you definitely want to do. Think about how you communicate best. Do you love being in front of the camera? Are you a whiz at writing clever and compelling blogs? Is your strong suit tracking down informative hard-to-find articles that relate to your business and then sharing them on social media? For the most magnetic results, focus on the kind of media content for which you have a natural talent and that best showcases you and your brand. By the same token, don't be afraid to train yourself in other areas so you can switch it up a little. At first I didn't know what to do in front of a video camera, but I learned, and now it's in the mix for my content.

### Don't Worry about a Weak "First Response"

As I said before, when you start out, it's easy to think that nobody cares about all the greatness you're putting out there. Don't sweat it. Your attitude toward your audience almost has to be, "Hey, if I keep going, I'm going to wear them down at some point. Eventually I'll say something that clicks, and they'll want to buy from me." You don't have any idea how long it might take. I can't tell you how many people on my newsletter list have said, "I've been reading these things for five years," and I look at them and realize, "Wait a minute. This person has never spent a dime with me." But even though they haven't, they're still *paying attention*. Because they stay on the list, many of them do eventually end up hiring me for private coaching or some other service. You just never know. But you'll never find out if you don't stick with it.

### *Accelerating Your Platform*

If your platform doesn't seem to be developing as quickly as you'd like, there are a few other ways you can boost its power and effectiveness. Here are four of them:

### Accelerant #1: Borrowed Authority

Whenever you can get the endorsement or participation of someone who already has authority with your niche, you receive some implied authority as a result.

For example, if, when I was a fitness coach, Arnold Schwarzenegger happened to stop by and tell one of my clients, "This Pat Rigsby? He is the REAL Terminator," well, that would have certainly rocketed my reputation with that person!

The same is true for you. If you can get someone who is a known expert or celebrity in your industry to participate in your platform, you can't help but look good—and gain some authority as a result. For example, I've participated in television shows and books that featured other more high-profile business experts. I did that because those kinds of projects put me on the same level as those folks, even if temporarily. I'm then able to point back to those projects to show potential clients the kind of company I keep.

## Accelerant #2: Writing a Book

Most people have never written a book and never will. They think anyone who *does* write a book must really be the real deal when it comes to expertise. Therefore, if you write a book, you will be automatically granted a certain degree of authority, even by people who never read a page of your book. Just knowing that you are a published author is enough proof of your credibility for them!

Yes, to an extent, this is silly. The world has no shortage of authors these days. The massive number of books published every year on Amazon is almost enough to convince you that everyone in the world *has* written a book (or maybe two or three). But don't let the numbers stop you. The fact is, publishing a book is still a quick ticket to attaining substantial authority. Even if you self-publish, it's still an impressive feat to become an author. In a way, a book is the most powerful business card you can have; it's a credibility tool that always does the job.

(By the way, you can create other information products that can also build authority for you, such as a DVD or online video instruction series. These can also be impactful.)

## Accelerant #3: Speaking Engagements and Seminars

Showing up and speaking in person is a great way to demonstrate your expertise and build up your personal brand. An in-person meeting with people creates the strongest kind of connection you can imagine. People feel like they know who you are and, just as importantly, they can find out how much you know through your presentation.

At the same time, you don't have to get too complex or sophisticated with your presentation or the information you provide. As you consider what to include in your presentation, be cognizant about your level of knowledge versus where your audience is in regard to your topic or area of expertise. The people filling the seats are most likely beginners at something in which you're an expert.

Now, not everybody has great public speaking skills. For my part, I used to be deathly afraid of public speaking. Then I realized that if I got over my fear, I would have another significant way to expand my platform. Keeping that in mind, I took over a weekly workshop. The first time I did it, I ended up drenched in sweat. But gradually I came to love it. Like anything else, public speaking requires practice, so put yourself out there and you'll improve your speaking skills (and comfort factor) rapidly.

**Accelerant #4: Outside Media**

When you make yourself a part of other people's media platforms, it takes you beyond your usual crowd, exposes you to new leads, and expands your reputation as a leading expert in your field.

Traditional media platforms still work, and they still have a bit more prestige than online news sites. They can be as small and localized as the town newspaper or as huge and worldwide as CNN. Whatever the venue or size, it's great if you're used in a straight-ahead news story as an authority on whatever they're talking about. People seeing that story will walk away with a higher opinion of you as a result. You might also look to be interviewed on TV or radio talk shows that need your kind of content. Admittedly, traditional media doesn't pack the punch it used to, but it still has a lot of cachet. I know on my street alone, at least half the people still have a newspaper sitting below their mailbox every morning. So what's the downside to getting myself in that newspaper?

New media—blogs, podcasts, online news/lifestyle sites— are what people are consuming more of today. If you can be a guest on someone else's popular podcast or contribute a column to a blogsite that gets a million hits, you will boost your name recognition and maybe motivate some folks to seek out your website and become part of your list.

### *Deposits and Withdrawals: The Currency of Relationships*

I've hit pretty hard on the idea that you must provide value to people on a regular basis. There's a reason for that. Every time you deliver that value, you're making a deposit on that relationship. You're earning credit. Having that positive on your side of the ledger creates goodwill on your followers' side. You're giving more than you're getting.

Some outfits, however, attempt to take more than they give. I'm sure you've encountered marketers and businesses who, once they have your name, begin a relentless campaign to separate you from your money. For them, it's all about flash sales and special deals. But those deals stop seeming so special when you're bombarded with them. After a while, you completely tune them out.

That's because those businesses are constantly making withdrawals from your relationship. They want it to be all about them making a sale, not you getting any real value from them. There's a negative on their side of the ledger, and there's no reason for you to want that relationship to continue.

With your platform, you want to connect more than market. You want to help more than sell. You want to keep their attention, not drive them away.

I can't say it more simply than this:

**IDEAL BUSINESS RULE #18: GIVE MORE THAN YOU GET, AND YOU'LL END UP GETTING A LOT MORE THAN YOU GIVE.**

# CHAPTER 11

# 3 MILLION REASONS WHY MY PLATFORM WORKS

3,000,000.

Yep, that number up there is three million. That's approximately how many words I've written during the past ten years for my daily email newsletter. That's a lot of words, and if I'd set out to write that many the task may have seemed overwhelming. But I never considered it intimidating because I composed those three million words one email at a time. I never had that kind of crazy goal in mind. Never in my life did I think I'd ever write three million words. But I've done it. And more importantly, it's paid off for me.

In this chapter, I want to talk a little about how I've made this aspect of my platform work like gangbusters for me and my business brand, and I also want to share a few of those three million words so you can get an idea of what I do and how I do it. It may not be what works for you...but it will give you an idea of how to build relationships that last (through value your niche can use).

### *The Daily Email*

Every single morning, including Saturday and Sunday, I send out an email to everyone on my list, a total of forty thousand people.

However, I don't write *for* forty thousand people. When I write each line of my newsletter, I approach it as though I'm talking to one single person in a casual conversation.

Also, I don't try to solve all the world's problems in that one email. I focus on one simple idea that has the potential to make my recipients' businesses or lives just a little bit better. Because I am offering that kind of positive content, I just might inspire them to read the next day's email to see what they will get out of that one.

By doing that every day, I build a lasting relationship with those who like what I say and want more of it.

Technically speaking, it's the simplest thing in the world: a short email, entirely text, no HTML. It's just like a note to a friend. I wouldn't worry about putting fancy graphics on a note to a friend, right? I just write in a conversational tone, nothing flashy. It feels personal. It feels real. It doesn't feel much like marketing to me or my readers.

But it is.

I don't come right out and ask them to hire me in the body of the email, but in a short and simple P.S., I do offer my services. But I make sure the balance always tips strongly toward offering value and making the connection, which, I believe gives me an advantage over the others who use their marketing lists almost exclusively as a transactional tool. To those kinds of marketers, their database isn't filled with people, it's packed with potential dollar signs. Of course, I want to make some sales as a result of my emails—but my attitude is to approach them as people with whom I want to build relationships, not just make a quick buck from.

To me, the perfect vehicle to build relationships is my daily emails. Here's the beauty of the era we live in right now: We have so much technology at our disposal that it makes it easy to reach massive numbers of people in a micro-second. Thirty years ago, I would have had to go to countless Chamber of Commerce events and speak to numerous other groups to get anywhere close to connecting with forty thousand people. Now, with email, I just click "Send" and it's done.

With that click, I strengthen my platform every single day. Through these emails, people get to know me and learn what I'm all about. They can see I'm consistent and dependable (after all, that email shows up every day), and they will recognize my authority because I share so many things I've learned. Eventually, that consistent delivery of valuable content creates the most essential element: trust. When those on my list develop that trust in me, when they realize I have something valuable to offer them, they feel confident about contacting me for help when they have a business problem.

And suddenly, I have a new client.

Want to know more about my philosophy when it comes to email marketing? Let me share one of my emails that deals with this very subject:

*During the past couple of weeks, I've been asked to share my thoughts about email marketing to several different groups of entrepreneurs.*

*Now, I'm not going to bore you with all the details of those presentations, but I thought it might be useful to give you some of the more important takeaways, knowing full well that I'm basically sharing what's probably my biggest competitive advantage.*

*See, I suspect that I view email differently than most people who use it as a tool to sell their products or services.*

*I think of it as simply a means of connecting.*

*I don't really think in terms of list size or content... and I certainly don't think of the people who are kind enough to give me their attention as transactions.*

*Back in my college baseball days, I recruited by making calls, sending notes, and meeting face-to-face. I wanted to connect with players, parents, and coaches in a way that fostered trust and hopefully led to the right players coming to be part of our program.*

*If a player chose to go somewhere else, I wished them well... knowing that our school wasn't going to be a fit for everyone. Sometimes those players who started somewhere else eventually decided to transfer and join us. (I don't really care about being the first choice... only the best choice:))*

*So when it came to "marketing" (if that's how we're defining my emails...I don't) via email...I pretty much just took the same approach.*

- *Try to connect. If you're willing to make the time to read what I write, I want to make your day a little better. Whether it's giving you a tip that helps your business, sharing a story that motivates you, or simply reminding you that you're not alone in this whole entrepreneurial thing. I want you to be happy you made the time for me.*
- *Treat the daily essay I write as I would a note to a friend... because that's what I want it to be. Now, I know that I'm not going to get the opportunity to meet everyone who reads this face-to-face, but I still recognize what many don't: I'm not sending my daily email to a list of tens of thousands...I'm sending it to YOU. We're all individuals, and I want to treat you and respect you accordingly. I need to make it worth your time and your attention.*
- *The "connection" part of what I write is way more important*

*than the "sales" part. Sure, I'm an entrepreneur just like you, but I know that if I do a good job of adding value to your life regularly, when I have something for sale that is a fit for you, you'll consider it. But I think most people approach it in the opposite fashion: they sell and then try to fill in the gaps with "content."*

- *As for that "content" thing, I don't really use that word when I'm describing what I try to do. To me, content is just another word for information. And I don't know that we need more information, so I want to deliver more than just information. I want to deliver help so you can simplify things. I want to make it easier to apply what you know. I want to deliver coaching, motivation, strategy...but not just more random information.*

*Obviously, there is more to my approach to email. But all in all, it's just not as complicated as most entrepreneurs seem to think it is.*

*Value people's time.*

*Be worthy of their attention.*

*Find ways to make their day better.*

*Respect each reader as an individual.*

*Write like you're writing to a friend...because, hopefully, you are.*

*Think of what you'd say if that person were standing in front of you...then write it.*

*Do those things, and you'll be writing better emails than me in no time.*

*Dedicated to Your Success,*
*Pat*

*P.S.—I get asked pretty regularly about teaching people how to build an email marketing system. If that's of interest to you, reply and let me know. I don't have something planned as of yet...but it's come up enough that I'd consider it.*

That's the kind of email I send out every morning (and you'll notice how I get my marketing message in my P.S.). I usually write it the day before and, again, I do this every single day of the week and have done it for the past ten years.

My email newsletter has become a huge business driver for me. There's not a week that goes by that I don't have somebody reply to one of these emails and write, "Hey, I've been on your email list for four years. I'd like to talk to you about coaching."

I've used my email system as the driver to sell over 250 franchises. Obviously I'm not selling a franchise through emails, but those emails are the catalyst. People reading them get to know where I'm coming from and discover that my philosophy and ideas are the right fit for what they want to do. They see I can address their specific business problems in specific ways.

Not long ago, I had a doctor who consults with NASA write to me and say, "You don't know me; a friend forwarded your email along to me so I got on your list. I just want you to know how much you're helping me and how much you're helping other people. You probably have no idea how much you're giving us all." I get these nice responses on a regular basis, and it motivates me to keep going.

Here's another one of my daily emails that's a little counter-intuitive. But that's what I think makes it interesting to my readers...

*One of the common things that I see thrown around is this concept of following your passion.*

*When it comes to building a business, I think it's a pretty bad idea.*

*Let me explain.*

*See, following your passion seems like a cop out to me. It's just not how things work in a practical sense for most of us...and it's not for the reasons you might think.*

*For most of us...what we're passionate about changes. As a young child, I was passionate about playing with trucks and drawing. In elementary school, I loved playing in the woods and baseball. In high school, baseball was still a passion...but I was interested in weightlifting, girls, and all the other "high school boy" stuff. I've always been an avid reader too.*

*What was I NEVER passionate about?*

*Business.*

*Writing.*

*Speaking.*

*But my current business is serving as a coach to entrepreneurs, primarily in the fitness industry...a career I never knew existed up until the age of 30.*

*So what's my point?*

*Three things, really...*

1. *I think business success is more about matching your strengths with opportunities.*
2. *We don't know what we don't know.*
3. *What we are excited about or passionate about changes over time.*

*Over time I got to blend my existing strengths and develop new ones and match them with a professional opportunity—helping business owners like you—whom I've grown to love.*

*Now was that me blindly following my passion?*

*Not a chance. Heck, much of my business has been built on writing... roughly three million words in the past eleven years.*

*I couldn't stand to write earlier in my life. But as I got better, I enjoyed it. Now I write every day and it's one of my favorite things I do. I didn't know that I'd like it eventually. I didn't know a career like mine could even exist.*

*So that's why I tell you to play to your strengths or to focus on your unique ability. Because if you are strong in an area and match that with an opportunity—or create an opportunity around those strengths—that's where success happens.*

*And that match is often something you'll come to love doing if you build your business the right way.*

*Make sense?*

*I hope so... because I want you to succeed, and simply following your passion oblivious to everything else won't make that happen.*

*Dedicated to Your Success,*
*Pat*

*P.S. If you'd like to work with me to build a business around your strengths, reply and let me know.*

## Be Real with People

By the way, don't be afraid to be a human being when you use these kinds of channels. By that I mean, it's okay to show your flaws or that you're vulnerable. It helps you connect to your similarly human audience.

For instance, here's one of my emails that's all about my mistakes:

*I often share things that have worked for me or have helped me grow my business, but today I wanted to share some of my biggest business mistakes for three reasons:*

- *If I can help you avoid the same mistakes, that would be awesome.*
- *It's fun to see how things are despite all these mistakes.*
- *Hopefully you'll see that you can screw up a lot and still build the business you want.*

So here they are in no particular order:

1. *Not putting in the work to get great at paid traffic (I'm ok, but not nearly where I should be and I'm remedying that now).*
2. *Saying "Yes" to too many things (there are plenty of good opportunities... but they're not all the right opportunities).*
3. *Overvaluing the things I'm not passionate about in business and overpaying to fill that void (things like accounting and project management are very important, but they're not things you give up equity to address).*
4. *Not investing for my kids or my retirement early enough (even when I didn't have much money, I should have done more because I had to play a lot of catch up.)*
5. *Not following my gut soon enough when it was time to change (twice I've felt like it was time to make a big career move about a year before I actually pulled the trigger... I should have moved faster).*
6. *Not focusing on my IDEAL Business a little sooner (I focused more on "big" than "IDEAL").*

7. *Thinking too small*

8. *Stepping back from going out and speaking and networking at events that weren't mine for a couple of years (those are always high ROI events for me, and I didn't spend enough time on them for about a thirty-month span).*

9. *Not supporting my clients, students, Masterminders, or Franchisees who went into business coaching soon enough (now it's one of the things that I'm most proud of).*

10. *Not spending more time on Holly's business.*

11. *Allowing myself to get pulled away from playing to my strengths from time to time.*

12. *Not sharing enough stories in copy or marketing (when I do, the message is better and it's more well received).*

13. *Occasionally letting my competitive side get the best of me.*

14. *Working with too many people who weren't a good fit.*

15. *Getting pulled away from coaching (now virtually everything I offer has a coaching component).*

16. *Not working with baseball in some way sooner (now I've got a couple clients who are "baseball guys" and I look forward to keeping that as a segment of whom I work with. I really enjoy it, so it should be there).*

17. *Taking too long to figure out who my Perfect Clients are.*

18. *Getting pulled away from my vision.*

19. *The times I've not been part of a Mastermind group (I always thrive when I'm around top-level peers).*

20. *Letting businesses become bloated (now it's all about what you keep... not what you gross).*

21. *Not always writing my best copy (I look back now and see sales letters that I know I could have increased conversions on by 25 percent if I would have put more time into them).*

22. *Spreading myself too thin...which led, in part, to #20 (I've owned over twenty businesses in fitness in eleven years. In hindsight that's too many :)).*

23. *Not doing enough with upsells (I've only done about 40 percent of what I should have and could have done with them, knowing what I know now).*

24. *Going through periods where I didn't spend enough time with the people I care about most outside of Holly, Tyler, and Alex.*

*And finally...*

25. *Settling for things being okay—I started a business to have the income, impact, and lifestyle I wanted...that's why I left coaching, so I could be more "in control" of that. But from time to time I settled for things doing "okay" in business (by the standards of what I want) because I had an awesome family, earned a nice income, and had accomplished more than I originally thought I could when I went into business in the first place. Now I know better.*

*You can build your IDEAL Business, but it's not going to happen without getting clear about what it is and settling for nothing less than getting there.*

*Hopefully these mistakes of mine will help you avoid some of your own :)*

*Dedicated to Your Success,*
*Pat*

### Drill Down on a Single Point

I'd like to share one more email with you to demonstrate how I try to "drill down" on one topic and use it to give value to my readers. I'd also like to leave you with this last thought when it comes to how you interact with your marketing list: The more real you are with the people on your list, the more you come to them on their level, the more accepting they will be of you—and the more they'll respond to what you're saying.

*I've had a good couple of weeks. I've gotten to speak to some really, really successful people... and every time that happens I learn something.*

*So one of the things that I've been reminded of in that span is that the most successful people don't try to be or do everything.*

*They master the few.*

*They have focus.*

*And that's different from being efficient.*

*In fact, I remember talking to one owner of a pretty big business who was consumed by efficiency. Everything needed to be more efficient. But the thing he was missing is illustrated in this Peter Drucker quote:*

*"There's nothing so useless as doing efficiently that which should not be done at all."*

*See, most of us spend great portions of our day trying to get better and do efficiently things that we shouldn't even be doing at all. Whether you call it your area of strength or your unique ability...that makes no difference. What makes a difference is that you spend about 80–90 percent of your professional time doing that stuff. If you can do that... you'll be so far ahead of everyone else; it won't even be competition anymore.*

*Your ability to focus on those things—your $100- or $1000-an-hour tasks that you do best and not get distracted by the $8-an-hour stuff or the stuff that might be good but isn't your focus—will move you more quickly toward your goals.*

*But it requires you to master a skill that few of us have.*

*That skill is the ability to say, "No."*

*In fact, I'll admit that this is probably my biggest professional failing.*

*See, Warren Buffet is an icon I admire. This is what he has to say on the subject:*

*"For every one hundred great opportunities that are brought to me, I say no ninety-nine times."*

*That's what he attributes his great wealth and success to… saying "no," ninety-nine out of one hundred times. I'm good at saying "no" to doing a lot of tech stuff or doing tasks that don't allow me to use my unique ability…but I'll be the first to admit that saying "no" to great opportunities is tough. It's something I really have worked on over the past couple of years. The willingness to say, "It's great, but it's not a great fit for me."*

*But this focus isn't just focusing on your unique ability or the ability to say "no" to tasks or opportunity. It's also about focusing on only offering what you can do better than everyone else. Deciding what not to do. What not to offer.*

*If you do a few things incredibly well and a few others are done in a pretty ordinary (or worse way)…just get rid of the stuff that's not up to your standards. See, success has less to do with what we can get ourselves to do and more to do with keeping ourselves from doing what we shouldn't.*

*So what does this mean to you? Well, look at your schedule. What are you doing that you should have said "no" to? Look at the marketing that you're doing that isn't working versus the things that are working well?*

*Can you pour the resources of the things that aren't effective into the things that are strong?*

*Think about how you're spending your time and your resources.*

*If you had to eliminate half of it, what would you cut?*

*Think about what you offer. Should some of it be eliminated? What about those clients or patients you don't enjoy? Can you get rid of them?*

*Now I know that you can't just go around saying "no" to this and eliminating that. Once you've opened up some bandwidth... then you just commit to doing fewer things extraordinarily well.*

*Stop trying to be good at everything. Start being great at a few things. My guess is that you already do it in certain areas of your life. You may outsource your automotive maintenance or putting a new roof on your house. You say "no" to doing a lot of things you could do already...because it's not what you could do, it's what you should do. So figure out what else you are willing to give up in order to get what you really want.*

*Then do it.*

*The most successful people I've met have all been willing to give up some things—the quest to be good at everything, opportunities sent their way, tasks that don't fit their talents—to get the outcomes they want.*

*It works for them, and it will work for you too.*

*Dedicated to Your Success,*
*Pat*

You don't have to send your content through emails, but you do need to have some vehicle to deliver value on a regular basis. Some people thrive as public speakers, but in today's world of Internet domination, you need to develop one online channel that you're a champion at, whether it's videos, blogs, emails, or even just short impactful tweets. Choose your medium and start connecting.

# CHAPTER 12

# IDEAL TIME MANAGEMENT

Okay, we've just spent a whole lot of time on business. Now, let's get back to real life—*your* life.

Sure, all the information I've shared in the past few chapters is important to your professional success, but your professional success should co-exist with your personal happiness. In my IDEAL Business model, entrepreneurs always pursue their professional goals and protect their personal goals. They know nobody else is going to do that for them.

The reality is, entrepreneurs are driven. For most of us, it can be really easy to lose sight of the clock and "keep on keepin' on" way past the time when we should have gone home for some R&R. It's understandable—we're passionate about what we do (and if you're not, you should probably sell out and become a nine-to-fiver).

However, entrepreneurs can also end up working around the clock, not because of passion, but because of the pressure that goes with owning your own business. You can start buying into the dangerous idea that if you don't stop working, you won't fail. That's a recipe for burnout.

Time doesn't have to be your enemy. You can make it your ally. You have the power to not only get done what you need to get done with your business, but also enjoy the kind of quality personal time it takes to build a fulfilling life outside of your work.

What I've learned through the years is that there's no glory in being busy for the sake of being busy. A big danger sign looms when you keep asking yourself, "How do I get it all done?" Because the answer to this one is relatively simple—you don't. If you're working endless hours trying to get everything done, you'll wear yourself down to nothing in the process. The trick is to identify priorities and tackle them in order. Some minor stuff might be left on the table, but the key word there is "minor."

I love the story about Warren Buffet's personal pilot. Unsure what he wanted to do with his life he asked Buffet for advice. Buffet told him to write down his twenty-five most important goals. The pilot struggled to finish the list, and when he did, he brought it back to Buffet who then told him to circle the five most important goals on that list. The pilot did as Buffet asked and returned, asking him what he should do with the remaining twenty goals.

Buffet simply said, "Throw them away."

The moral of that story is that not everything can be a priority. We can't tackle twenty-five goals at one time. Even ten is a big stretch. You've got to focus on what truly matters, and that's the key to being efficient with your time and getting done what's most important. If you don't get to dust the staplers, you'll survive.

It all begins with looking at time from an entirely different viewpoint. The quote that sticks with me on this subject comes from the great personal development guru Earl Nightingale who said, "You can't manage time. We all have the same twenty-four hours in the day. What you can manage is *activity*."

In the next few pages, I'm going to provide some practical advice on how to deal with every business owner's biggest challenge: time. These won't be the usual boilerplate time management clichés (so don't worry about that). Instead, I'm providing hard-won lessons that I've learned from my own experience trying to do too much at once—and realizing I had to change my ways before it was too late.

It all comes down to this:

## IDEAL BUSINESS RULE #19: MAKE YOUR LIFE A SUCCESS, NOT JUST YOUR BUSINESS.

### *The Periodization Program*

With my fitness clients, I used a methodology known as *periodization* that allowed them to use a year-round training schedule to reach peak performance at certain intervals. They had to change up their workouts to make sure they weren't going too hard too fast toward specific fitness goals. Otherwise, it could be a disaster for their physical power.

The same holds true for an entrepreneur's mental and physical stamina. If you don't know when to let up, when to call for the cavalry and when to go full-throttle, you could burn yourself out too quickly. Obviously, there will be times that are stressful and difficult, but if you're feeling that way almost every day of the year, you're heading for trouble. That's why periodization is a great tool for time management for every entrepreneur.

In the fitness world, periodization is based on three time cycles of differing length:

- The Macrocycle (the big, overarching period, usually a year).
- The Mesocycle (usually a few weeks that focus on one specific aspect of training, such as muscle mass or aerobic capacity).
- The Microcycle (typically a week or a group of training sessions to accomplish one specific task).

I think you'll find this to be a great template for managing your IDEAL Business, with some simple modifications. For entrepreneurs, the periodization cycle breaks down like this:

- The Macrocycle represents a year.
- A Mesocycle represents a business quarter.
- A Microcycle represents a typical day.

Here's how you can work with these three planning periods in your IDEAL Business.

## The Macrocycle

The **Macrocycle** represents your annual plan, and here's where I probably break with most time management experts. You see, I don't believe in putting that much actual planning into an annual plan! Don't get me wrong, yearly planning is important, but because a year is a relatively long period of time; a lot of unpredictable things can happen in a year that can knock your strategies off-balance.

I prefer to focus more on scheduling than planning. I block out on the calendar the days where I know certain things are going to happen, both personally and professionally. From a personal standpoint, I plug in holidays, vacations, and any other important personal matters that will take me away from my business. Then on the professional side, I plug in my company's major calendar-based items. For example, if your business is very seasonal, block out your busy weeks and your not-so-busy weeks. If you have some regular annual marketing or promotional pushes (or if you want to start some), block those out as well. In addition, note what week you need to begin preparing for these occasions and create some deadlines for phases of any campaigns you plan to implement. Also, make room for continuing your education in your field. Are there seminars or conventions out-of-town that you should attend? Do some research and see how those dates line up with the rest of your year.

In general, your Macrocycle plan for the year is mostly about scheduling events you *know* are going to happen—or *want* to happen—in a twelve-month span. You hopefully know when you want to take time off, when you'll be swamped with business, and when you want to make a big marketing push. Schedule them so you know when to work toward them and when you have to work around them, if need be.

## The Mesocycle

My approach to **Mesocycle** quarterly planning, in contrast, is more like other people's approach to annual planning. This is where I like to get more into productive, goal-oriented thinking. My focus is on making each twelve-week period count in a significant way.

Why do I aim for goals in the Mesocycle rather than the Macrocycle? Because I find that going for them in a shorter, more compressed period motivates me, and I end up accomplishing more. When you're building toward a goal over an entire year, it's very easy to lose your momentum—that's why so many New Year's Resolutions fall by the wayside. It's typical for someone to say, as February rolls around or even March, "I still have plenty of time. I'll get started later." After all, you still have three-quarters of the year to get to it. But when there's always "later," you either never do or you get to it too late.

The same kind of thinking happens with year-long business goals. We get all fired up in January to make a fresh start, but a few weeks later, we find ourselves drifting away from our grandiose objectives and end up doing things in the same way as we've always done them.

With twelve-week planning, it's not so easy to do that. With that kind of focused time period, you might easily accomplish what's difficult to pull off in a year simply because of the different perception of time. There's more urgency to get to your goals before the end of the Mesocycle because you can always feel the clock ticking. When that quarter is over and you've done what you set out to do, you're going to feel relieved and enjoy that end-of-the-year feeling. With this system, however, you get to enjoy it four times a year!

## The Microcycle

In contrast, each **Microcycle** is about maximizing each *workday* to fulfill different kinds of mandates. Each one of those workdays should be about something specific.

The daily grind can be brutal if you don't handle it correctly. Most people will tell you their days are overloaded with stuff to do, they never have a moment to breathe. And yet a recent study by Salary.com discovered that the average person wastes *nearly an hour* of every working day.[1] A big culprit? Social media. Facebook disclosed that people in the U.S. spend five hours a week on Facebook alone![2] We can *say* we're too busy, but I honestly don't believe that's the case.

My attitude is this: We're not too busy; we're just not on schedule. So let's talk about getting on schedule.

## Getting into Your Zone

Benjamin Franklin said, "If we take care of the minutes, the years will take care of themselves." There's a lot of truth in that, and it completely applies to Microcycles. If you really want your days to be highly productive, start by micromanaging your minutes and really looking at how you're spending your time.

---

1. Aaron Gouveia, "2014 Wasting Time at Work Survey," Salary.com, Accessed September 28, 2017, http://www.salary.com/2014-wasting-time-at-work.
2. Sarah Frier, "Facebook's Second-Quarter Revenue, Profit Tops Estimates," Bloomberg.com, July 23, 2014, https://www.bloomberg.com/news/ articles/ 2014-07-23/facebook-posts-second-quarter-revenue-profit-topping-estimates.

## Productive Microcycles

I want to take this back to my old business, fitness, one more time. Sometimes, when you're working out, you get in a groove and time flies by. You're not thinking *about* what you're doing— you're *just doing it* (to paraphrase the famous Nike ad slogan). When your head is in that kind of zone, you get a lot more done because you're focused on and completely into the task at hand. That always feels good.

But how do you empower yourself to get in the zone with your business? What's the best way to unleash all your entrepreneurial energy in a productive way and create the kind of results you love to see happen?

For me, it all comes down to dedicating each day to something different and avoiding letting your flow get interrupted by a hundred other random tasks. You want to engage in results-oriented activities that move the needle—activities that grow your business and help you prosper—and you want to do that at the highest level.

Ideally, the goal is to commit at least 80 percent of your time to these results-oriented activities during what I call a *production day*. Doesn't matter if these activities involve networking, marketing, or directly tweaking your products and services, they're important, and they deserve your full attention. When you block out a day for them it allows you to get into the "productive zone," versus jumping back and forth between production tasks and support tasks. That kind of skipping around takes away your attention and negatively impacts your production efforts.

Dedicate at least two to three "microcycles" (i.e. days) a week to producing. Stay in your productive zone on those days and focus on what helps your bottom line. Use your quarterly goals and your annual scheduling to determine what you're going to be doing on those days a few weeks in advance, so you have time to

THE IDEAL BUSINESS FORMULA

think through what you're going to do and, more importantly, how you're going to do it. That way when you do hit those production days you're good to go and ready to get into your zone.

## Support Microcycles

Support Microcycles are days designed to make your production days much more, well, productive. This is when you can take some time to prepare for production days by doing research, making sure someone you need is available for a project, or setting up any other resources you'll need then.

Support days should also be used for administrative and back-office tasks. If you're still pretty much a one-man band, things like bookkeeping will end up happening during support microcycles. These days may be kind of boring, but when you commit a full day to getting admin tasks completed, you'll be more highly motivated to follow through rather than let those activities drag out and potentially interrupt a production day.

Another important item that should be on the agenda for your support days? Making sure your production days stay clear by delegating and outsourcing things you don't need to be doing yourself. As your business grows, you'll want to start building a team that can help you clear some duties off your plate. Because delegation only works if you take the time to train people properly or hunt down professionals (like accountants and lawyers) that can fill in some gaps, you'll need to take time to find and equip the people who will help you become even more productive.

You can't do everything yourself, and you don't want to. When you are playing to your strengths, you become acutely aware of the things you aren't great at. Here's the good news: There are people in your organization or outside of it who are going to excel at tasks that you barely manage to get done competently. No offense to your abilities, but obviously an experienced CPA is going to do your books better than you could. Part of your challenge as a business owner is keeping your head clear to be as productive as possible, so increase your delegating and outsourcing to complement the growth of your company.

## Non-Work Microcycles

Time off is critical to your success and critical to your IDEAL Business. First, it keeps your batteries charged. Second, you want a life beyond your office door. That's why it's important to schedule your time off in a way that gives you the most relaxation and allows you to get the most out of it in terms of getting refreshed and enjoying your life.

With that in mind, when you take time off, work toward getting to the point where you're taking a *full day* off. You don't want to go into the office for a couple of hours and then take the rest of the afternoon off. When you do that, you put your mind into a work mind-set that's hard to shake. Just as it's hard to stay productive when other trivial tasks keep coming at you, it's almost impossible to completely relax when you haven't made a complete break with your business.

What I like to do is take the complete day off from the time I get up to the time I go to bed—no work-related activities. I don't even read business books. How can I read a business book and not start mentally applying its contents to my own company? I can't!

Nor do I check work emails on my non-work microcycles. If you're at the beach with your wife and kids it's hard to stay focused on your time with them if you're constantly checking your phone and dealing with incoming work texts and emails. You end up not really being there with your family; instead, your brain is whirring, working on the incoming messages and wondering how you're going to handle what you're being told. To really recharge, and to maintain meaningful connections with the people you love, you've got to get away from your business.

Bonus: when you're refreshed you'll be better at your business.

Believe it or not, learning how to relax can be hard work. Some people actually get coaching on how to goof off! If you've spent your adult life as an entrepreneur who never stops, you might not know what to do with yourself when you're not on the job. You only learn by scheduling time off and planning for it.

It comes down to this: If you schedule time for a client, why wouldn't you schedule time for you? Make sure your personal life is as full as your professional one to really achieve life satisfaction.

## Keeping Time

Here are a few more nuggets of advice that can help you keep your schedule on track.

### Don't let emails and phone calls rule your life.

This, to me, is a huge rule. Schedule a block of time during the work day for emails and calls, and stick to it. Don't check your phone or your inbox every time you take a little break.

Yes, we live in an era of instant communication, but you don't have to instantly respond to every communication you receive. Being in constant contact with everyone can be a monster of a distraction and can really cut your work flow to a trickle. If you can avoid it, don't open your email until after lunch. For me, the morning is when I'm the most productive, and I don't want anything to get in the way of using that time of clarity and focus. I don't believe I have to answer an email on someone else's timetable—many times, I don't respond for hours or even a day or two. Same with calls.

You can't stay in the zone when you can't quit your phone.

## Limit your social media.

Social media has its place. It's important for marketing and for keeping in touch with your family and friends. But it also can eat up a lot of your time—up to seven hours of the week for most people. When you get on Facebook (or whichever platform you like to use) do it within a scheduled block of time, and don't go past that block. Or take five- or six-minute breaks to check it out. Don't spend hours randomly scrolling through newsfeeds, or your day will quickly get away from you.

## Make time for fitness.

This is something I know firsthand from my own experience: The healthier you are, the more energy you have—energy to put into your business. It's easy to neglect your body and skip working out when you're a busy entrepreneur. Short term, you'll get away with it. Long term, it'll catch up with you. Maintain your physical fitness and you'll find you have increased stamina to tackle your business challenges.

## Avoid eating in front of the computer.

Lunch breaks are important; they help you do better throughout the rest of the day. You'll get more stuff done by taking a walk, reading, taking the dog for a walk, whatever it is that helps you clear your mind and regain your mojo.

## Try a weekly review and planning session.

Accountability is crucial to any business, not just an IDEAL one. That's why I recommend an end-of-the-week review and planning session. For mine, I schedule ninety minutes every Friday morning, and I consider it the most important hour-and-a-half of my week. During that time I review what I've accomplished that week and whether I've met my goals. I then get into specific planning for the next week to make sure I can continue making the right kind of progress.

So that's how I do it. I admit not everything goes according to schedule. What in life does? But as with all of the ideas in this book, I consider it essential to have systems in place to keep me on track. When something throws a monkey wrench into those systems, it's relatively easy to get them (and myself) back up and running.

Time is a precious commodity. As with all precious commodities, you should treasure it.

# CONCLUSION

# THE IDEAL FUTURE

My guardrails are still very much in place. When I travel and I'm going to be spending more than two nights in one place, I make sure part of my family is with me. When I book meetings and speaking engagements, I do it around my family's schedule, not the other way around. Last year alone, our family took eight vacations, some of them shorter than others, but it was time spent exclusively together.

As I write this, it's about to be spring break for my kids. So I'm going with them to Orlando, Florida, where I'll host a coaching group there for a couple of days. But for the other five? We'll all be at Disney World. There won't be any early morning business calls to interrupt our time off, like that Thanksgiving weekend I wrote about in the intro to this book.

It's actually easier for me to continue to build professional success when I'm balancing it with my personal satisfaction. Maintaining an IDEAL business forces me to do things a little differently and think out of the box. Today, I'm a master at consolidating the things I need to do so I can get them done quicker—and eliminating the things I really don't have to do.

I'm more efficient. I'm more productive. I'm also a whole lot happier.

Now, it's not all rainbows and candy. I still have to go to my accountant and try to figure out complex tax issues. I must still dedicate quality time to my clients and keep up with current business trends. I must still make sure I'm doing a good job motivating and leading my team. And I have to deal with my own screw-ups because sometimes I make strategic decisions for my business that don't always work out. Usually they do, but it's not like I'm batting a thousand. I've never seen anyone with a perfect record, and whoever says they do…well, let's just say I'm skeptical.

So yeah, I still work hard. I still write my daily email, I still give my clients my all, and I'm still hopping on airlines to go speak here and there. But here's the difference: I used to spend 20 percent of my time doing the things I'm best suited to do. Now? It's 80 percent.

That *huge* improvement only happened because I put my guardrails in place. I put the ideas in this book into action. I didn't lose myself in busy work. To the contrary, I streamlined. I offloaded the tasks that weren't in my wheelhouse onto more qualified people and eliminated business ventures that were just not a fit for where I saw myself going.

In other words, I *made* my life happen instead of letting it happen to me. If I hadn't consciously decided to improve my quality of life, I don't think it would have improved—ever. But I chose to focus on my unique picture, what success looked like to me. I saw where I wanted to go—and that's the way I headed.

It's tough to break out of our daily routines. We get into ruts and don't realize that we possess the power to climb out of them. Does it take effort and thoughtful intention to change our patterns and habits? Maybe a little disruption? Yes, it does. But that kind of work beats just getting up, slogging through another meaningless day, and coming home so exhausted you're unable to enjoy your home life.

Sometimes my guardrails get a little dented. Earlier in this book I told you about how I made a point of never missing any of my kids' ball games. Well, you know what? I still ended up missing two games. Some business things got scheduled before my kids' game schedule came out, and I had to honor my commitments. *That* my children can understand.

But if I were to miss half of all their games? They'd be hurt, and I'd feel unbearably guilty.

So is everything *truly* IDEAL for me? No. Life doesn't work that way. Not even an IDEAL Life. But I know if I don't shoot for that goal, I won't get anywhere close to it. I've never been happier or more satisfied with my life, and I've never had a better relationship with my family—or my friends, for that matter. I've had the same best friend since the fourth grade and, for the first time in a long time, we actually have time to hang out. That wouldn't have happened if I hadn't created a better work-life balance since he lives three hours away.

Aiming for the IDEAL Life takes willpower. It takes determination. It takes direction. All of that must come from you. I think the last rule sums it up nicely:

## IDEAL BUSINESS RULE #20: IF YOU DON'T DO IT FOR YOURSELF, NOBODY ELSE WILL DO IT FOR YOU.

I hope you, too, can enjoy the fruits of pursuing the IDEAL Life as I have.

## About Pat

In the past decade, Pat Rigsby has built over 25 businesses as a CEO and Co-Owner, with seven becoming million dollar or multi-million dollar ventures. Two of those businesses, Athletic Revolution and Fitness Revolution, have been multiple time winners on the Entrepreneur Franchise 500, with each being the #1 franchise for it's respective market. Another business, Fitness Consulting Group, was a multiple time honoree on the Inc. 5000, placing as high as #580 on the list of fastest growing businesses in the U.S. Pat has also been a Best-Selling Author® 11 times over, presented keynote speeches in front of thousands of entrepreneurs, and has been featured in *Entrepreneur, Forbes, Men's Health, USA Today* and on hundreds of other media outlets.

When it comes to sales, Pat has personally sold as many as 116 franchises in a single year, and he's been the strategist and copywriter for over 10 million dollars in online sales (for his own businesses and millions more in sales for his clients).

Pat's coaching & consulting clients have been featured in places like *Men's Health, USA Today, Men's Fitness, Shape, Women's Heath, Huffington Post* and on ABC, CBS, NBC and pretty much any other media outlet you can think of. In addition to that, they've built some of the most successful businesses and brands in every corner of the industry, from local business and supplement companies to online businesses, certification organizations and even became Best-Selling Authors®. In fact, many (if not most) of the experts providing business coaching in the fitness industry have been Pat's clients, customers or franchisees.

The best part of this? Pat has been able to do all of these things and more while working from home, coaching his kids in baseball and soccer and enjoying a type of entrepreneurial lifestyle he would have never thought possible just a few short years ago.

If you'd like to see how you might be able to work together with Pat, you can reach him at pat@patrigsby.com.